D0622689

CAN WE BE GOOD WITHOUT GOD?

AN EXPLORATION OF BEHAVIOUR, BELONGING AND THE NEED TO BELIEVE

Robert Buckman M.D., Ph.D.

with many invaluable contributions by Michael Schulman

Illustrations by Martin Nichols

VIKING
Published by the Penguin Group
Penguin Books Canada Ltd, 10 Alcorn Avenue, Toronto, Ontario, Canada M4V 3B2
Penguin Books Ltd, 27 Wrights Lane, London W8 5TZ, England
Penguin Putnam Inc., 375 Hudson Street, New York, New York 10014, U.S.A.
Penguin Books Australia Ltd, Ringwood, Victoria, Australia
Penguin Books (NZ) Ltd, cnr Rosedale and Airborne Roads, Albany, Auckland 1310, New Zealand

Penguin Books Ltd, Registered Offices: Harmondsworth, Middlesex, England

First published 2000

1 3 5 7 9 10 8 6 4 2

Printed and bound in Canada on acid-free paper ♾

CANADIAN CATALOGUING IN PUBLICATION DATA

Buckman, Rob
Can we be good without God?: an exploration of behaviour, belonging and the need to believe

ISBN 0-670-89222-X

1. Ethics. 2. Religion and ethics. I. Title.

BJ1012.B745 2000 170 C00-931618-3

Visit Penguin Canada's website at www.penguin.ca

To James and Matthew, because thinking,
discussing (and also laughing) are
such important parts of life

Beliefs do not work because
they are true, but [are] true
because they work.

—William James (1842–1910)

William James, author of *The Varieties of Religious Experience* and much else besides, was a psychologist who studied the role and function of religion and religious ideas as part of the human mind. He clearly had very strong theistic ideas himself, yet his whole attitude was dispassionate and objective. All of his writings are centred on the theme of this quotation, although this particular phrasing of it comes not from William James himself but from the entry about him in *Chambers Biographical Dictionary*. Since it epitomizes everything that James said about the phenomenology of religious experience, I thought it was an apt epigraph for this book, and that it was fair to attribute it to him.

Table of Contents

CAN WE BE GOOD WITHOUT GOD?

INTRODUCTION

In the Beginning . . .

THIS BOOK IS BEYOND BELIEF

This book is not a debate about the existence of God. It's about something much more important than that.

What you're going to read here is a discussion of the ways in which belief in a god or gods has changed human behaviour and human history. We're not going to discuss what gods do for humans, we're going to look at what humans have done (and do) for the sake of their gods.

The connection between what we believe and how we behave is very complicated—and an exploration of even the simplest of the concepts involved can rapidly get bogged down in contradiction and obscurity. For example, take the simple word "good." Is there any general agreement among all the various communities and religions on this planet as to what constitutes "being good" and what doesn't? Reluctantly, we are forced to answer no. As a species, we are not even close to reaching a consensus on that definition. Yet, despite the lack of any universally agreed upon concept of good, as *individuals* the great majority of people do have clear and definite opinions as to what they regard as good and what as bad, and for most people those concepts are firmly rooted in their own personal religions.

Most of the world feels that the idea of good can only come from a concept of god, and you can't have one without the other. (As I'll discuss in more detail in a moment, "concept of god" in this sense means "concept of an external supreme intelligence that has designed and now controls the universe"). So the generally accepted rule, or working hypothesis, for most people is that you cannot be good without god.

Now although it is very difficult to argue with the *theory* behind that stance (the proof of god's existence or non-existence is always going to be elusive), we can discuss its *practice*, which has always been both troubled and troubling. To put it mildly, it is a disturbing fact that we humans, throughout the history of our species, have always been ready to kill and torture other humans in the name of an eternal and everlasting deity that (in most religions) encourages humans to love and tolerate one another. The two central ideas of being good and of following god have often been widely separated in practice.

This book is subtitled "an exploration" and it is exactly that. It is really a logical progression, a "thinking through" of the subject, rather than an instruction manual or a textbook. It offers a perspective on the connection between behaviour and belief—the connection between ethics and religion—rather than some sort of sermon or dogmatic tract. Which is perhaps no bad thing, since the world seems to have rather too many preachy instructional manuals as it is. Information and opinions from many different sources—philosophers, historians, neuroscientists, physicians, ethologists (who study behaviour), anthropologists, ethnologists (who study culture) and novelists, as well as my own views—focus on the deceptively simple question of the link between "good" and "god." Some of these views and observations are already known but many are brand-new, and they have never been assembled together in a single book before. I think you'll find that the ingredients make an interesting mixture, and that the result is both fairly coherent and enjoyable—even if you happen to disagree with some of it.

So, let's begin with three of the most famous words in the history of human belief: "In the beginning . . . "

The starting point for this "thinking-through" process—

the true beginning of "in the beginning"—is the human activity that we call "believing." And the first undeniable feature of the act of believing is a simple one: humans have always needed to do it.

As a species we have shown consistently throughout our history a powerful urge or drive to believe. We have always behaved—and we still behave—as if we need a set of cast-iron fundamental beliefs to act as a solid foundation for making sense of the world. Even the most cursory glance at our history demonstrates that point. At every stage of our evolution, human beings have stoutly upheld firm beliefs in some overall plan or organizational design for the universe. We have never functioned as conscious and thinking creatures without some form of that belief. What is interesting is that the designs we have believed in have almost always included a powerful and indefinable Something at the centre: a Something that created the entire universe, gives it momentum and controls it on a day-to-day basis.

If you'll forgive some all-inclusive generalizations, there are basically four central tenets or principal assumptions at work (with the vast majority of religions—and therefore of humans—subscribing to all four). They are:

- First, that there is an overall plan or organizational design for the universe;

- Second, that the plan was set in motion and has been influenced or controlled by one or more external deities;
- Third, that this plan includes the destiny of individual humans, and entails rewards or punishments meted out during life and after death, based on the individual's behaviour;
- Fourth, that the rules of good (i.e., proper, moral, ethical) behaviour have been set, as part of the overall plan, by an external god or gods.

Whether there is (or is not) in reality an external deity at the centre of everything is not really the focus of this book. For the purposes of looking at the factors that affect human behaviour, it is not that important whether there really is or is not a god. It is much more important to look honestly at the *effects* of believing in a deity, and at what those beliefs have done for us and to us. So let's start by talking about the different things that human beings believe in, and then go on to look at how those beliefs have influenced and changed the way we humans have behaved in the past, and the way we behave now. At the end of that process we might be a bit closer to answering the questions, Is belief in the four main tenets described above actually essential—is it *truly* necessary—in order to be "good"? Or can you be good even if your belief system doesn't happen to have a god at its centre?

When you think about it objectively, the connection between, on the one hand, an external deity who has created and now controls the universe, and, on the other, the little details and everyday trivia of human affairs might seem a little tenuous. But actually, in most people's minds, they are intimately and immediately connected: God-the-external-deity has a big say in human destinies, and humans have to believe in a deity in order to behave decently. That point is made in almost every discussion on this subject. Sooner or later when people are talking about the connection between good and god somebody will protest, "If you don't believe in god, you cannot believe in anything." By which they mean or imply that if you don't believe in god and therefore his/her/its commandments and precepts, you cannot possibly behave decently and ethically, and also that you cannot experience love or show compassion or humanity. In fact, they usually go on to say, if you don't believe in god, then you're not much better than a soulless robot or mechanical android, only a little more sentient than a vacuum cleaner, or words to that effect. Yet, of course, that presents only one side of the argument—it is not a proven conclusion. In fact, it raises the question to be answered and provides the reason for this book's existence in the first place.

Now it is quite possible that at this moment—while you're reading this page—you have your own personal answer to the question quite clear in your mind. In fact, you might even be thinking to yourself that the answer is so clear to you that it's not really worth your while going through the process of re-examining the issue. Let me assure you that this is not the case. I predict that you are going to find the process of thinking through this issue enjoyable and stimulating, and that after reading this book you will feel that you have gained in several ways, and that your time and work were not wasted. (If not, then I humbly apologize in advance!) Examining the foundation and the basis for our beliefs is never a wasted effort. And while we are talking about reassurance, let's take a break for a "lack of hazard to your spiritual health" warning.

A LACK-OF-HAZARD WARNING

If you happen to have a strong personal belief in an external deity, please let me reassure you that this book is not a veiled attempt to convert you. Examining and discussing various options and alternatives in religious matters is (honestly!) no more threatening or dangerous than the process of looking at options and alternatives in politics. When you come to think about it, in the political arena everyone is accustomed to the idea of one political party making up the government while several other parties argue alternative views and opinions. In fact, we usually think of a multi-party, multi-choice parliamentary system as being intrinsically better, fairer and more equitable than a dictatorship or a one-party system.

The comparison of politics to religion is a fair and useful one. The existence of a few people—a minority—who do not believe in god is not a threat to the great majority who do, any more than the existence of a small opposition party is a threat to democracy itself. In fact, the opposite is more usually true. A nation generally does very well if it nurtures an atmosphere in which political discussions and votes are open and free. In the same way, religious discussions are improved by an honest consideration of the alternatives. If you can compare the conduct of human matters to a parliament (not an unreasonable comparison, actually—on good days and on bad days!) then, in matters of belief, those who don't believe in the existence of god are simply a minority opposition party. They offer an alternative to the governing party but are still contributors to the system and not opponents of it. So whatever your religious belief at this moment, please rest assured that this book does not represent a threat to your own system of values. In fact, examining the foundation of your own faith might actually help you to define and strengthen what it is that you really believe and the reasons for it.

WHAT ARE WE TALKING ABOUT HERE? A FEW DEFINITIONS

Words mean different things to different people. The word "god" can probably be used in hundreds of different ways, so in order to set the ground rules of this book I'll need to make it clear precisely what I'm talking about.

A lot of people use the word "god" to mean something outside human beings, "something out there." "God" in that sense means an *external* intelligence, a motive force that has an existence independent of human beings (in other words, if all human life were extinguished, god would still exist). For the purposes of this book, and in order to remove any ambiguity, "god" will refer to an "external god" or "external deity." Since this is the sense in which the word is used most commonly, I shall also use the word "theist" to specifically mean those who genuinely believe in an external deity. Similarly, to identify those who do not believe in an external god, I shall use the word "non-theist" (atheist).

Of course, not everyone uses the word "god" to mean

something external. For lots of other people the word is used to describe something internal and personal—a resource, a source of energy, an essence that provides guidance and inspiration and comes from within. What is central to this concept of god is the idea of transcendence. By touching and using this inner resource, the person sees beyond and progresses beyond—transcends—the normal limitations of daily human thoughts and emotions. The word "god" in this context implies a way for the person to make contact within himself or herself with an inner resource. God, in this sense, is similar to the concept of an inner experience that we express with the words "spirituality," "soul" or "holiness." So for the sense in which with the word "god" is used to describe that internal central human force or essence, the "god within," I'm going to use the word "spirituality."

Using the two terms—external god and spirituality—to define and distinguish between these two (among many) different senses in which the single word god is often used will make at least some of the issues less ambiguous and easier to discuss.

Then, there is the small matter of defining what we mean by the word "believe" (or, to paraphrase an ancient British professor, "what we believe we mean by the word 'believe'"). Here's a simple, practical definition: belief is any set of perceptions sustained by a person as a consistent attitude or view that extend beyond any factual information available, or even persist contrary to relevant factual information.

Not all beliefs have anything to do with religion (although, obviously, all religions and religious experiences contain a central element of belief). Beliefs may be entirely secular and non-religious. Some people believe they have a surefire system for winning at roulette; others have a good-luck charm or a talisman that they sincerely believe in; others believe in astrology, palm-reading, numerology and thousands of other different secular systems. All of these beliefs meet the criteria above and so fit the definition but are not, of course, religious or spiritual in nature.

One further comment by way of closing this introduction: this book doesn't just ask questions.

Almost anyone can write a book setting out the fundamental dilemmas of human existence. It is not very difficult to do that—in fact, it's particularly easy when we're talking about dilemmas of faith and the contradictions of religion in a modern world. I'm not going to stop there. In this book you will find some proposals for trying to answer these questions. In the final two chapters, I'll show you some of the ways that ethics (or morals) and religion can be separated: how we can think about the different religions (and about the absence of religion) in a reasonable and equitable way, and how a code of ethics can exist without a deity at its centre. So, if this book does stir up questions about some of your previously held tenets, beliefs and thoughts, it will at least offer you some serviceable ways of thinking about the solutions.

HOW THIS BOOK IS ARRANGED

Obviously, belief and behaviour merge into each other: much of our behaviour is affected and moulded by what we believe, and many of our beliefs are based on (or are altered by) our past experiences, including our own behaviour and other people's reactions to it. This makes it difficult to draw a clean and clear line between the two. Even so, for the purposes of this book, I shall try to do that. In the four chapters that make up Part One, "Believing," I look at the human activity that we call believing. In Chapter 1, I examine the origins of belief, and then in Chapter 2 look at the act of worshipping, and at the heroes, gods and other figures that have become objects of worship. In Chapter 3, I describe some of the many benefits that the act of believing provides for the believer. Then in Chapter 4, I detail some contemporary neurological research and hypotheses concerning the origins of those beliefs—how we experience belief, and which parts of the brain are involved in that experience.

Part Two is entitled "Behaving," and I start, in Chapter 5, by looking at the usefulness of existing codes of behaviour when they are (according to the believers) handed down to mortals from on high. That chapter therefore includes the advantages to the community—the upsides—of religion-based codes of behaviour. Chapter 6 illustrates some of the downsides: the problems and disadvantages created by theistic belief. In Chapter 7, I set out some of the alternatives to god-given codes of behaviour—other ways that we all can aspire to being "good." In Chapter 8, I suggest some techniques and methods by which we can use some of these principles to produce more constructive behaviour.

So let's begin by looking at what human beings gain from belief in an external god—how those beliefs evolved and how they work.

PART ONE

Believing

CHAPTER ONE

Belief: A Very Brief History

THE PERSONIFICATION OF "BECAUSE"

How did belief begin? What did the earliest human beings think and believe when they first began doing both of those things? Well, of course, the subject matter of humankind's earliest conscious thoughts and beliefs will never be known accurately; we will never know for certain what our early ancestors—*Homo erectus* and prehistoric *Homo sapiens*—were actually thinking about as they developed thought itself. But we can make a few informed guesses using archaeological evidence about the habits of humankind, the histories of human societies and the existing beliefs of remote communities, those relatively untouched by contemporary development.

CAUSALITY: WONDERING "WHY?" AND SEEKING A "BECAUSE..."

As soon as humans became conscious of themselves and

conscious of the world around them, it is probable that they tried to create logical explanations for the events that they saw taking place in the world. As a species, we seem always to have started our thinking process with a "Why?" This seems to be the first true thought when a human becomes conscious of an event in the world. In modern language, the thought would be something like "This event has just happened: what was this event connected to, in order to make it happen?" or, in other words, "This has just happened. Why?"

The search for some form of cause to explain everything around us seems to have been a prerequisite for any form of ease from the perplexities of the world. The moment you start asking "Why?" you feel uneasy until you find something that resembles a "Because . . ." You could say that the act of wondering always begins with a "Why?" It is the verbalization of inquiry, and it seems obvious that our versions of a cosmogony—a theory of how the universe began—and the legends of the gods involved in that process started out as accessible expressions of "Because . . ." That *because* was an involuntary subconscious search for an antidote to the unease caused by *why*?

What I'm suggesting here is that humans are drawn—by reflex or instinct or inbuilt drive—into making connections of causality between events in the outside world, assigning causes and prime movers to explain those events. Early humans created a chain of causality at first to explain the happenings they saw around them, and later to explain the origins of the cosmos, and this brought them comfort.

BELIEF—THE FIRST 100,000 YEARS (OR SO)

The first line of evidence to support this hypothesis is fairly obvious in even the most superficial glance at human history. In every race, culture and religion, we *all* ponder the causes of events, and we have clearly done so ever since the beginning of recorded history. There is no civilization on this planet that does not have stories, myths and legends explaining causes of natural occurrences, and these stories go back as far as their records go. Pondering, and then trying to establish causality, is clearly an inbuilt human trait.

Relics providing evidence of belief are among the oldest artifacts found in any human culture. What we know about *Homo sapiens*'s first 100,000 years or so (just about our entire time on earth thus far) is based on what has been found buried in the earth or in caves. Human bones, stone tools, the vestiges of the animals and plants that people ate, traces of dwellings and artworks both carved and painted have yielded valuable clues as to how our ancestors perceived the world around them.

Even more valuable clues were provided by the discovery, as explorers made their way into the world's most remote areas, of hunter-gatherer societies that were still living in ways that the earliest modern humans lived. These were (and still are in some cases) basically egalitarian communities of one hundred to two hundred people with no fixed address, moving from base camp to base camp with the changing seasons in search of the wildlife and vegetation that provided their food.

Anthropologists tell us that these sapient people in so-called primitive societies (a politically incorrect term but a useful one) did not perceive themselves as the only truly conscious creatures in the world. They were animists, and for them consciousness was everywhere—everything around them had its own consciousness, its own spirit. Similarly organized communities nowadays uphold the same ideas, perceiving animals, for example, as conscious (today's Inuit still thank the sea mammals they hunt for willingly giving up their lives). Many hunter-gatherer societies, in their creation myths, trace their own origins to conscious animal ancestors, identifying their family-clans by their ancestral animal totems.

Not only are all other forms of animal life perceived as being conscious, but all of nature: trees, rivers, mountains, clouds, winds, the sun, moon and stars (vestiges and derivatives of this animist notion survive today, for example, in the still-prevalent belief in astrology). Finally, dead people were held to possess consciousness, in the form of a spirit that survived the body's dissolution. When some intrepid Australians ventured into the interior of New Guinea in the early twentieth century, the indigenous people took the visitors for their disembodied dead ancestors.

Early humanity was faced with trying to make sense of a confusing, often unpredictable and dangerous world. What caused illness and death, and how could they be avoided? What caused fertility—women to conceive and crops to grow—and how could fertility be ensured? What caused the daily alternation of day and night, and how could the sun be encouraged to return each dawn? What caused the yearly succession of seasons, and what guarantee was there that if winter came, spring would be close behind? What caused the rain, essential for agriculture, and how could one avoid sustained drought? What caused the annual migrations of fish, birds and mammals, and how could they be made to come back each year?

The answers our ancestors found were based on the idea of universal consciousness—intelligent spirits residing in each and every aspect of the world. Before there were gods, the world was full of spirits. Before the gods took up residence on the tops of mountains, in the depths of rivers or above the sun and the moon, people prayed to the spirits inherent in the mountains, rivers, sun and moon, along with the spirits of the animals, plants, winds and departed human ancestors. Special members of the society, shamans, would make contact with these spirits, to learn what the spirits wanted in exchange for health and fertility.

Steadily, societies developed from the small egalitarian communities of semi-nomadic hunter-gatherers to larger, more hierarchical settlements of urban herders and agriculturists (a transition that began in various parts of the world about ten thousand years ago). As that occurred, the egalitarian animist construct in which *all* nature was imbued with spirits also became more hierarchical. This is probably when the first gods were born (or, more likely, goddesses—nearly all of the earliest figurines found in caves, at burial sites and on excavated altars are female).

Elaborate stories explained how the gods and goddesses influenced the most vital aspects of health, climate and fertility—in large part stimulated by fear of natural catastrophes and disaster—and that was the origin of religion. Religion began as the personification of the *because* as a spirit or god or animus that held the key to the universal *whys*. If humans had never wondered *Why*? there would have never have been any gods.

We have two main sources of information about the workings of religion in relationship to nature. First, with the development of writing, along with the proliferation of artworks depicting people making sacrificial offerings to the gods, we begin to see archaeological evidence. Second, many anthropologists and folklorists, particularly in the Victorian era, studied legends, rituals and religions in undeveloped areas (at the time) of the world and analyzed their significance and role.

These are well-travelled waters. This particular line of inquiry has been energetically and elegantly pursued by hundreds of authors and investigators in the past. I am going to discuss a few of the studies that I've found most accessible and intelligible, written by people who have illuminated and clarified this area rather than being simply dogmatic or (worse!) merely emptying their research notebooks of endless minutiae without actually sorting them out.

ANIMISM AND THE FEAR OF NATURE

Humans have always been afraid of nature, and they have every reason to be.

As far as early humans could see, terrible and inexplicable things were always happening (and, in my opinion, still do). If humans were looking for *because*s to answer their *why*s, a high proportion of their most urgent *why*s would have come from sudden natural catastrophes. It is highly likely that beliefs were first and most urgently pressed into service to answer the anxieties raised by this fear of natural events. William James, the American psychologist of the late nineteenth century who analyzed the role of religion in the human psyche, put it neatly in referring to the old saying that "the first maker of the Gods was fear." However, James, who was also a philosopher, did not undertake a methodical examination of humankind's beliefs. That type of work was the domain of anthropologists and folklorists, people who studied and compared rituals, beliefs and behaviour in various areas of the world.

Of that type of work, the earliest immortal classic on the relationship between humankind and nature (as the former became conscious of the latter) is Sir James Frazer's 1908 compendium, *The Golden Bough*.

Frazer was a Victorian anthropologist and folklorist who combined his fascination with humankind's early beliefs with some serious thinking and brilliant insights into what makes humans tick. He was a Cambridge graduate who, during his extraordinary and productive career, looked at the world's folk legends, superstitions, beliefs and religions. He distilled much of it into *The Golden Bough*, an analysis of the major types of legend and ritual and how humans create around them a model of what they imagine goes on with their gods in the various heavenly realms. Frazer describes all kinds of rituals, ceremonies and superstitions and analyzes their symbolic functions: how they attempt to explain events in the world in a tangible and accessible form, and to encourage beneficial outcomes.

To early humans, as I've said, the world must have appeared to be a pretty terrifying place. There were unexpected gales, rains, floods, predators, droughts, eclipses and so on, and the beliefs of animism were invoked to provide the *because*. According to the animist belief system, everything had its own life force, its own intelligence and its own self-determined plan of action. Not just animals and plants, but even what we call inanimate objects had their own agendas and their own schemes. Storm clouds decided when to break and on whom to rain. Mountains decided when to strand voyagers. Rivers decided when to flood. Sun and moon obeyed their own whims in deciding when to emerge and so on.

The Golden Bough is full of detailed accounts of rituals, most of which are examples of animistic belief, practised by various peoples, countries, cultures or groups as they tried to make the world run in a more beneficent and predictable way. After humans stopped being totally nomadic and started cultivating crops, they needed to make sure that the following year's harvest would be a good one. So there were rituals and ceremonies to ensure that the spirits or gods of weather, fertility and crops did their stuff. Many rituals were centred on the sun, moon, wind or rain. For example, the Sencis of Peru had a ritual in which they shot burning arrows at the monster that appeared to be eating the sun during a solar eclipse. Similarly, some tribes of the Orinoco had rituals that involved burying burning brands used for lunar eclipses.

Lithuanian worshippers of Perkunas, the god of thunder, would sacrifice oak trees to get good crops. Frazer also details a large variety of corn god rituals. For example, the Mandans and Minnitarees of North America had a ritual involving offerings of dried meat to a spirit of the corn called the Old Woman Who Never Dies. Similarly, the Romans would sacrifice a horse annually on the fifteenth of October after a chariot race on the field of Mars and use the blood (and some body parts) to encourage a good harvest.

Other rituals were much more dramatic, or even downright macabre. The Dieri of Australia, as Frazer describes, had a ceremony to encourage rain: "Two wizards, supposed to have received a special inspiration from the Mura-mura [spirits] are bled by an old and influential man with a sharp flint and the blood . . . is made to flow on the other men of the tribe who sit huddled together. The blood is thought to represent rain."

Rituals to encourage crops in some places even involved human sacrifice. Frazer reported a sacrifice of a

Sioux girl in 1837 by Pawnees, on instructions that were believed to have come from the Morning Star, carried by a certain bird sent as a messenger.

Whatever the ritual or ceremony, however, as spring usually *did* follow winter and the crops *did* grow, the practitioners came to the conclusion that these rituals were pretty effective, and they were soon regarded as being essential. Animism and the rituals it required seemed to be quite reliable.

What worked for the fertility of the fields was also applied to the fertility of humans. Rituals and ceremonies to guarantee conception were just as important, and almost as varied. For example, the god Osiris was regarded as a crucial factor for guaranteeing fertility of all kinds of living organisms, including humans. One hymn to Osiris proclaimed that the world waxed green in triumph through him, and another that "thou art the father and mother of mankind, they live on thy breath, they subsist on the flesh of thy body." To which Frazer adds: "We may conjecture that in this paternal aspect he was supposed, like other gods of fertility, to bless men and women with offspring, and that the processions at his festival were intended to promote this object as well as to quicken the seed in the ground."

In all these religious ceremonies, there were two assumptions regarded as unarguable: (a) that the events that were the focus of the ceremonies were controlled by external deities, intelligences who decided the destiny of the worshippers, and (b) that the deities could be (and should be) propitiated—in other words, by going through the ceremony, the people would earn the favour of the deity, who would then grant them the outcome they were asking for. You could call it special pleading, you might even call it bribery, but it was really a form of bargaining: "We will do this in the hopes that you [the deity] will do that."

What becomes quite clear from these accounts is the way our species thought about natural phenomena. When some natural event appeared to threaten or harm them, or when there was a natural event that was desirable, they devised rituals to intercede with the controlling forces. All over the planet, people prayed for rain. They prayed in their own language and in their own way, using formulas and symbols that made sense to that community and that acted as a cohesive force, binding members of the community to each other. Yet in all of these observances, the central element was constant, a contract with the deities: "We'll do our bit, so please do yours." Animism imbued almost every force that we now call natural with intelligence and wisdom—and it was a great success. However, there were more types of spirits and gods than the everyday ones that inhabited and motivated every visible physical object in the world. There were the unseen ones, too.

FEAR OF THE DEAD

Many researchers in this area, Frazer included, identify another major motive force underlying intercessionary prayer: fear of the dead. It has always been a fundamental belief of most people that when a person dies, not everything to do with that person dies with him or her. The animus or the soul or the spirit is believed in many cultures and religions to live on after death. In some religions, it was generally assumed that most immortal spirits were benevolent and helpful to the living, and sometimes the bones of the deceased were cleaned and brought back and kept in a place of honour in the home. However, in many more religions the spirits of the dead were thought to be highly powerful and dangerous, and potentially malevolent. They needed to be placated and propitiated.

Frazer gathered reports on this aspect of early religions from all around the world.[1] He quotes dozens of examples in which a people's religion included, or was founded on, the belief that the spirits of their dead ancestors were the gods or spirits controlling the everyday events of the living. Prayers, sacrifices, libations and all kinds of offerings are

1. In his book *Fear of the Dead in Primitive Religion*, first published in 1933.

listed. For example, the Kiwai of New Guinea used to leave offerings of food and coconut milk on graves at the start of the turtle-fishing season with the incantation "Give us turtle: we give you food." If the fishing was bad, a fisherman would go to his father's grave and say, "We have cleaned your grave and given you a drink. Come with us." After that, they thought the fishing would be good. As with the advent of spring every year, so with the fishing—success was proof of the reality of the spirits. Since eventually the fishing *would* be good, the action of repeating the ceremony until luck changed would always prove the power of the spirits.

In many religions there was no clear distinction between the spirits of dead ancestors (who were basically omnipotent) and gods. Our ancestors believed in that, and so they were afraid of the souls of *their* ancestors. That fear was a major factor in shaping their early religions. The spirits of dead ancestors needed to be placated and to be granted peace, which required special and specific ceremonies—and special and specific people to perform them.

THE PRIESTS OF INTERCESSION: MEN FOR ALL SEASONS

Now, the sense of a divine presence (whether or not related to the spirits of the dead) watching over and controlling human destiny demanded some organizational changes in human communities.

Communication with divine forces soon became something of a privilege—not everybody was allowed to communicate freely, and on his or her own behalf, with the deities. Shamans, priests and other religious interpreters and ambassadors rapidly arose and became a prestigious class in early societies. The power of the shaman or of the priest depended on the assumption that the gods were powerful, and on the desire of the people to ask the gods to intercede on their behalf using the shamans or priests as the legitimate conduit for their requests.

The need to believe is such a strong force in human behaviour that the power vested in the priests became truly enormous. The hierarchical structure and power of organized religions today attests to the deeply felt need to communicate with the deity using those who have particular talent or training in the process. The deities needed a sturdy conduit, and it is no coincidence that the word "vicar" is derived from the root meaning "representative of" (as in "vicarious"). Power coming from above humans required power among humans as a distribution network.

Hundreds of authors have detailed different forms of these religious structures in the past, and have deduced the evolution of those religious systems from what they have observed. But there is one other source of evidence about the evolution of religious beliefs *in our own times*, and it is a fascinating and important episode in the history of human belief.

NEW RELIGIONS IN OUR ERA: CARGO CULTS

The last line of evidence in this chapter showing how humankind invents gods to cope with the unknown is perhaps the strongest of all—and it is a modern line of evidence that is totally free of conjecture and guesswork.

Even in our own era, human societies have invented new religions and systems of supernatural beliefs to explain the apparently inexplicable and to intercede with what they have believed to be divine beings. The evidence lies in the existence of some strange religions known as "cargo cults," which evolved during the late nineteenth and twentieth centuries in the Pacific islands of Melanesia. These cults offer a unique insight into the ways that humans develop legends and rituals to explain and to control the unknown.

What happened is this. Until they were colonized by Europeans, the people of the islands of Melanesia had essentially been untouched by western-style civilization. Once the Europeans arrived, their traditional ways of life were seriously disrupted. The natives were coerced into harsh, underpaid labour on plantations and in mines, and Christian missionaries told them that their beliefs in their old gods and ancestral spirits were false and sinful.

What was even more significant to them, however, was their first experience of western material goods. Colonial officials and planters regularly received amazing and apparently miraculous goods, which arrived in large (and perhaps supernatural) steamships. The indigenous people wondered why their own gods and ancestors had denied them these astonishing things, and they developed a complete system of myths and legends to explain this.

They realized that the white people who received the goods—the officials and the planters—did not actually make the goods themselves. Furthermore, whenever any of the machines broke down, they had to be sent away to be repaired, which made the indigenous people think that the officials and planters were incapable either of making or of repairing the goods. They came to believe that these material goods were actually being created by spirits, and they decided that the creators were their own ancestors, who had died and were now living in a volcano on another island and making these wonderful goods for their descendants. The white people had therefore stolen or appropriated these magnificent products that were actually intended for them, the natives of the islands.

One of the most famous of the cargo cults began in the village of Vailala, New Guinea, in 1919, and quickly spread to nearby communities. The wave of bizarre behaviour that became known as the "Vailala madness" was based on a prophecy that a steamship, operated by the ancestral spirits, was on its way with a cargo of food, tobacco and weapons for the native Papuans, but in order to receive it they would first have to drive away the whites. Their old ceremonies were obviously no longer effective and so they were now denounced as wicked. Ritual masks and other sacred objects were consigned to bonfires. Existing food supplies were destroyed, crops were abandoned and all plantation and mining work halted in the belief that the cargo accompanying the soon-to-arrive ancestors would end forever any need to work. Many people simply sat motionless.

New temples were erected that looked like small-scale models of European buildings. Poles were set up in imitation of flagpoles and radio antennas. Bibles were "read" by trembling, twitching, illiterate natives who preached about a god who wore a coat, shirt, pants and shoes. One prophet claimed to have visited and returned (after three days!) from the land of the dead ancestors with a new set of rules and rituals. The impending arrival of the steamer was repeatedly predicted, and each time it failed to appear on schedule a new arrival date was prophesied. There were also repeated rumours of the steamer actually having appeared (elsewhere, of course). In at least one case, local natives had to be forcibly prevented from storming a trading vessel and seizing the cargo, which they considered rightfully theirs: the white crew, they insisted, were their dead ancestors.

The Europeans, concerned about the natives' refusal to work and the threat of violent rebellion, arrested the cult leaders. In most villages, when the supernatural steamer continually failed to arrive, the inhabitants finally gave up and chopped up the simulated European buildings and furniture for firewood. The "madness" gradually began to fade, and the natives returned to their ancient ceremonies—as well as to the mines and plantations.

New cargo cults developed during the Second World War, particularly when American planes began to use previously unvisited islands as temporary airbases. Riches arriving from the sky appeared even more godsent than material arriving by sea. A well-known—and still active—example of these more recent cargo cults is the one devoted to John Frum.

John Frum is a mysterious figure whose name first appears in 1940 in the records of the colonial administration on Tanna, one of the islands that make up the nation of Vanuatu (formerly the New Hebrides). No one has been able to identify who Frum was, or indeed if such a person ever existed. He is supposed to have come to Tanna by airplane during the 1930s with the power to speak and understand all languages. When he left, he promised to return with a bountiful cargo, ushering in an earthly paradise. First, however, the natives would have to reject the Christian missionaries, expel the whites, spend or throw away all their money, kill their pigs and neglect their gardens. Frum would then provide everything they needed.

A wide range of beliefs about John Frum have since developed. He is variously described as big and strong, short and slight, white, black (with fair hair), living in the United States, living in a volcanic crater on another island, the reincarnation of an ancient deity or of a powerful tribal ancestor. At various times, natives have appeared on the scene claiming to be Frum himself or one of his sons, or insisting that they have received orders directly from either Frum or a Frum son.

Published accounts describe how, to show that they were prepared for Frum's return, the natives built an airfield for him to land on. They equipped it with a wooden replica of an aircraft to adorn the landing strip and a wooden hut to serve as a control tower, in which a native wore two wooden earphones with bamboo antennae.

They also built a radio tower with tin-can speakers strung from wires to allow him to speak to his people.

Every February 15—the day his followers believe he will return—they hold a ceremony with offerings of prayers and flowers. His repeated failure to appear has not dampened their hopes. As one Tanna resident told a visiting *Toronto Star* journalist in 1999, "Christians have been waiting 2,000 years for Jesus Christ. We have been waiting only 60 years for John Frum to come back. Why are *we* the ones who are thought strange?" (A reasonable question when you come to think about it—and not an easy one to answer.)

As further evidence of the evolution of new beliefs, the people of Tanna also believe in the supernatural powers of other figures. After Britain's Prince Philip visited the island in 1974, he too became the focus of a new religious cult. He is believed to be, like John Frum, a holy reincarnated ancestor-spirit destined to return someday laden with bounty.[2]

The cargo cults of Melanesia clearly evolved as purposeful religions, dedicated to showing the supernatural powers or deities that their worshippers were worthy of

2. One is reminded of the Roman emperor Claudius who was astounded to be told that in some far-flung outpost of the Roman Empire—a little town called Colchester in England—he was worshipped as a god. Deification that happens while the subject is still alive must be the highest form of flattery!

receiving the magical commodities previously available only to Europeans, and that they would welcome the return of the spirits and their planes (or ships) bearing the cargo. Eventually most of the cargo cults died out as colonialism waned and awareness grew as to the real source of the manufactured goods. But their rapid development, format and rituals provide an extremely important insight into the way belief springs up to help explain the unknown—and to try to influence it to the worshipper's advantage.

Cargo cults are not merely exotic anthropological curiosities. The beliefs and rituals that we see are not just a strange and alien form of behaviour pursued by a people so totally different from ourselves that we can maintain a comfortable objective and ruminative distance. Quite the opposite.

Cargo cults are important symptoms of the way the mind works when confronted with perplexing features of the outside world. We are easily prodded into erecting a system of beliefs. It is clearly something that humans do: when confronted with events far beyond their initial understanding and experience, they invent stories to explain those events, and then they believe those stories. It is a universal way of gaining comfort. Building a system of *because*s quells the anxieties we feel when we meet a bunch of *why*s, and the cargo cults are contemporary evidence of that mechanism at work.

Furthermore, the analogies to various religious forms, beliefs and rituals of the developed world are not a coincidence—they are also telling us something. They are telling us that humans have a deep urge (you might almost call it an instinct) to create models (literal or metaphorical) of what they most wish for, and then invoke a deity, invested with supernatural powers, a deity who they hope can be propitiated and who will reward them for their devotions.

The rapid appearance of these new religions shows how readily and quickly that happens—how readily humans ascribe unknown events to deities, and how quickly they can develop a system of beliefs and devise ceremonies and rituals to earn reward from those deities.

SUMMARY: THE NEED TO BELIEVE

Humans have always been propelled into forming a set of beliefs as part of their way of dealing with the world—and in particular as part of the search for a *because* to answer the millions of *whys*. Belief is a fundamental part of the human approach to the world: in our history it has always been a prominent feature of our way of making sense of the world. In that respect, it is justifiable to call it an urge or even an instinct—it is so deeply ingrained in the human world-view that it is part of the characteristic way of forming thoughts and views that we call "human."

I am aware that in making this suggestion I differ from earlier authors and earlier conventional wisdom. Throughout most of recent history, until the last few decades, it was taken as a given that belief was a conscious and rational choice, a decision made by consenting adults after considering the alternatives. For example, William James, in his 1898 book *The Will to Believe*, asserted that belief is a matter of conscious choice and is an act of will—even though his argument actually supports the opposite view. James—who had deep religious convictions of his own—was fighting a rearguard action against what he regarded as a somewhat effete tendency to become fashionably atheist. He was convinced that belief could only be arrived at by a process of choice and will. William James would not have enjoyed reading this chapter—but then he would probably have been totally flummoxed by the cargo cults. Even so, I feel that I am on very firm ground in proposing that the drive to believe is a deep urge and not a conscious choice or act of will.

In the rest of Part One of this book we shall be analyzing how and why that deep-seated need to believe so often settles on an external deity. We shall start by looking at the process of deification—of making gods out of heroes or out of legends or fables. To start that exploration, in the following chapter we shall look at the fundamental relationship between humans and our legends and myths, and at the ways that we place persons, objects and ideas at the centre of them.

CHAPTER TWO

Worship: Creating Gods in Man's Image and Heroes in Gods' Images

> So long as men worship the Caesars and Napoleons, Caesars and Napoleons will duly arise and make them miserable.
>
> —Aldous Huxley (1894–1963), *Ends and Means*

WORSHIP: HEROES, GODS AND OTHERS

Having established that we all (as a species) share a deep-seated drive to believe, we can now look at a different aspect of humankind's beliefs: worshipping, and the need to identify figures, persons or objects worthy of worship. It is an activity that humans seem to be particularly good at.

It seems clear that as a species we've gone in for worshipping as part of the implementation of our beliefs since the very origins of civilization, and I shall start by looking at some of the ways this phenomenon has been analyzed. We all relate strongly and immediately to stories, legends and myths, so a logical place to begin is with their central figures: how they become magnified and exalted, imbued with divine powers if they are human heroes and (usually) imbued with human failings if they are gods.

Since our society's frame of reference—the way we look at the subject—has shifted quite dramatically over the last century, it is best if we begin with the world-view of worship in the mid-nineteenth and early twentieth centuries.

OLD-STYLE HEROES: BORN, NOT MADE

Until recently, people didn't think very much about heroes—they were simply there. They were a feature of the landscape, as one might imagine that most Nepalese admire and respect the Himalayas but don't spend every day wondering what the land would look like without them or how they came to be there in the first place. Heroes and the act of worship were aspects of daily life, they were fixed points, they were a given. The first major popular work about hero-worship emerged in the nineteenth century—and actually, it was not really a work about hero-worship at all, it was much more a work *of* hero-worship. It was published in 1840 by the Grand

Historian and the Great Explainer of the Victorian era, Thomas Carlyle. He put hero-worship on the map (though not quite in the way he intended). In any discussion of the act of worshipping, we are almost duty bound to start with Carlyle, if only to identify a point of departure and to demonstrate to ourselves how far we have progressed since, and in a different direction from the one he charted.

Carlyle was a diligent and extraordinarily prolific writer, sometimes a great thinker and occasionally a philosopher. In 1840, he published, based on a series of his lectures, the world's first major analysis of heroism and hero-worship, his classic *On Heroes, Hero-Worship and the Heroic in History*.

If Carlyle were writing nowadays we would label him a "pop psychologist"—albeit an extremely serious (and almost humourless) one. What he was trying to do was to explain the world—and particularly the tide of history—to the general public. He wanted to be (and was for decades) the author of the Definitive History and Analysis. He wanted to pin the world's events down like butterflies in a museum display, spread out and fixed forever, dictating the unalterable and correct view of whatever topic he focused on. He wrote as if there could actually be a complete, permanent and definitive account: history written "the way it was."

Carlyle was a hard-working, self-made man at a time when there was a widespread sense of confidence and security in the natural order of things (including the justifiable rise of hard-working, self-made men). Most historians and writers believed, as he did, that there was such a thing as a Universal Truth that encompassed everything—including all aspects of history, nature, science and morals. Most of them believed that with enough diligence, research and effort, the Universal pattern could be captured and set down, and Carlyle was a true product—and propagator—of that spirit.

In attempting to analyze and define what it is that makes a hero, he made his starting point quite straightforward: he believed that some people—a very small number—were stamped with the mark of true greatness, and that they had certain qualities that inevitably set them apart from the common person. He believed that truly great men were born, that the qualities of greatness could not entirely be made, and that "history is the biography of great men," as he put it. His view—in this respect similar to Friedrich Nietzsche's concept of the *Übermensch*, the superman—was that heroes exist almost as a separate species, a rare breed, and that they inevitably rise to occupy the pedestal they deserve. He gave no space or credence to the idea that heroes could be merely "men of the moment" or that they could as easily be created by social forces and opportune timing as by inherent greatness. He would have totally and utterly disagreed with the quotation from Aldous Huxley at the top of this chapter. Carlyle's opinion was straightforward and simple: it was the hero that created the circumstances—not the circumstances that created the hero. In his view, heroes were "the leaders of men, these great ones: the modellers, patterns . . . of whatsoever the general mass of men contrived to do or attain." The "movers and shakers," as we would say nowadays.

Carlyle divided hero figures into six categories: the hero as divinity, as prophet, as poet, as priest, as man of letters (a nod in the direction of his own endeavours, perhaps) and as king. In each category he attempted to define those qualities that made the person a hero and what it was that revealed the stamp of true greatness. Carlyle's analysis was a major success at the time and it set the tone on this subject for decades, so that remnants of it still lingered on until the end of the Second World War.

There are many good and important lines of reasoning that can be taken from Carlyle. He pointed out, for the first time, as far as the general public was concerned, humankind's predilection for worship. In the very selection of the mixture of heroes that he chose, he demonstrated that the *activity* of worship is the common factor. His cast of characters is interesting and eclectic. Among the divinities, he chose Wotan/Odin, the pagan and the Norse gods. In the category of prophet, he wrote a warm and sympathetic account of Muhammad. Among poets, he picked Dante and Shakespeare; among priests, Luther; among men of letters, Johnson, Rousseau and Burns; and among "kings," Cromwell and Napoleon. He shows that all worship shares similar characteristics, whether the object of that worship is a human hero, or a god, or a hero who later becomes a god. In this paragraph, for example, Carlyle lumps together Odin, Jesus, Voltaire and Johnson as objects of worship:

> Yes, from Norse Odin to English Samuel Johnson, from the divine Founder of Christianity to the withered pontiff of Encyclopaedism [Voltaire] in all times and all places, the Hero has been worshipped. It will ever be so. We all love great men: love, venerate and bow down submissive before great men: nay, can we honestly bow down to anything else? Ah, does not every true man feel that he is himself made higher by doing reverence to what is really above him. No nobler or more blessed feeling dwells in man's heart.

And that's the important point: the act of worship elevates not only the object of worship but also the worshipper, which is why it is such a pleasurable and rewarding activity.

Carlyle was something of a groupie for heroes and fame. Among all the praise and adulation, he never drew any clear lines between fame, glory, genius, heroism and godhead. To him, the figure at the centre of each hero-legend was there because he (almost always a *he*) was, well . . . a hero. Yet by the very act of choosing his subjects, he demonstrated something of major importance—humans create heroes, and heroism can be found across a continuum that runs from ordinary mortals to gods. Heroes were frequently the offspring of the coupling of a god or goddess with a mortal. Many heroes became gods at the end of their earthly life or career (Wotan, for example), and several other humans were thought to have ascended directly into heaven from earth. Conversely, many gods visited the earth in the guise of heroes (or sometimes in other roles to test the perspicacity of mortals). That continuum—the spectrum extending from mortals through heroes to gods—was in many respects a classic Victorian world-view. It assumed that there was a divine natural order, one handed down by God, and that the officers and executives of that divine plan were the great men, the heroes.

Carlyle demonstrated how deeply we all hanker after a hero figure who has superhuman powers and who will sort out the various sorry messes of our lives. And his book on hero-worship was in itself an act of hero-worship. In the process of considering heroes, we ourselves create them.

In Carlyle's view, the heroes were heroes because they were made of different stuff, of heroic material. And what was the definition of heroic material? Most people in the late nineteenth century, including Carlyle, felt that heroic material was revealed if the person became a hero. It was really a circular argument, a self-fulfilling prophecy, and it ignored completely the role of the public's attitude—the role of the people who elevate the potential hero from the level of the commoner to the heights of hero. That part of the equation was never even considered by Carlyle, or by anybody else in the Victorian era. It would be more than a hundred years before someone would come along to state plainly (and in a popular style accessible to the general reader) that myths, legends, gods and hero-worship are all phenomena of the human way of seeing the world and coping with it. The man who achieved that was Joseph Campbell.

MANKIND AND MYTHOLOGY: A RELATIONSHIP THAT GOES WAY BACK

We all know that myths and legends are powerful stuff—particularly because our minds take them in so quickly and deeply. Almost instantly, these stories mean something to us and become part of our view of the world. Of course, they don't depend on truth or factual content for their power, and the depth of the impression they make—"it might have been thus"—is just as powerful as—perhaps more powerful than—"it was."

By far the clearest thinker on this subject was the wonderful Joseph Campbell (1904–1987). Campbell was the world's greatest authority on myths and mythology. He was a scholar, teacher (beginning in 1934 at Sarah Lawrence College) and writer, and his name became widely known to the general public shortly after his death, when a series of interviews with the broadcaster Bill Moyers was made into a television series, "The Power of Myth," in 1988. However, his extraordinarily deep understanding of mythology and his phenomenal and detailed knowledge of the world's legends and myths had been widely known and respected in the academic world long before.

In his groundbreaking book *The Hero with a Thousand Faces*, first published in 1949, Campbell sets out a wide-ranging yet scrupulously detailed analysis of mythology and humankind's attachment to it. He points out that myths are part of the fabric of human understanding—which is why, as he said, we get the same feeling of contact and recognition from an Inuit fairy tale and from the sonnets of the mystic Lao-tzu. It is the image, legend or fable that we seem to have known before and now recognize. Campbell shows that in anthropological terms, myths are at their most useful at particular stages in our development—phases of transition for which they form part of the rites of passage: birth, naming, puberty, marriage and death.

However, he went on to show that there is a common, almost constant theme underlying many superficially different myths. The underlying theme is that of the saviour, the hero and conqueror of evil forces, and Campbell compares the legends of literally dozens of them (Theseus, Prometheus, Osiris, Gautama Buddha, Jesus, Cuchulainn, King Arthur, Herakles, Krishna, Gilgamesh, Maui and many others).

The role of the hero-saviour is to change the old world order to the new, and his journey resembles, to some extent, life's rites of passage. Campbell points out that there are three salient stages of the process. First, he emerges from obscurity (or at least from "the outside"). Second, he undergoes a struggle with vast forces, during which he achieves an epiphany (metaphorically, as Campbell puts it, he "dies to the past and is reborn to the future").

The examples of that second stage—the epic conflict—are legion: Jacob fighting the angel and creating Israel,

Jesus battling Satan in the desert, Jonah in the belly of the whale, Herakles fighting the sea monster, Finn MacCool and the monster *peist*, Maui swallowed by his great-great-grandmother Hine-nui-the-po and all the Greek gods with the exception of Zeus swallowed by their father Kronos. Many religions share more specific themes and images within the category of epic struggles: Campbell points out, as one example, that crucifixion is common to several of them, including the legends of the Norse god Wotan:

> The pagan Germanic divinity Othin (Wotan) gave an eye to split the veil of light into the knowledge of this infinite dark, and then underwent for it the passion of a crucifixion:
>
> *I ween that I hung on the windy tree*
> *Hung there for nights full nine*
> *With the spear I was wounded, and offered I was*
> *To Othin, myself to myself*
> *On the tree that none may ever know*
> *What root beneath it runs.*[1]

1. From Joseph Campbell, *The Hero with a Thousand Faces*; the poem quoted by Campbell is from *Poetic Edda*, "Hovamol," trans. Henry Adams Bellows (New York: American Scandinavian Foundation, 1923).

The third stage involves a rebirth, new beginning or resurrection (also an event common to a large number of religions)[2]—the hero brings to the world the benefits of the wisdom or enlightenment he has gained. As Campbell shows, the constant theme of this voyage or journey underlies a vast number of legends and provides the consistent link between the saviour and the notion of resurrection common to so many legends, histories and religions.

What all the myths exploring this theme have in common is very important: they all illustrate humankind's very deep longing—almost an ache—to be rescued. We all yearn for redemption, the deep, primal hope that whatever our current problems, there is somebody out there who will come in and rescue us. The ultimate longing, of course, is for salvation from death, the hope of

2. This is just a small example of the breadth of Campbell's knowledge and research: "Throughout the ancient world such myths and rites abounded: the deaths and resurrections of Tammuz, Adonis, Mithra, Virbius, Attis and Osiris . . . are known to every student of comparative religion: the popular games of the Whitsuntide Louts, Green Georges, John Barleycorns and Kostrubonkos, Carrying-out-winter, Bringing-in-summer and Killing of the Christmas Wren have continued the tradition in a mood of frolic into our contemporary calendar; and through the Christian church (in the mythology of the Fall and redemption, Crucifixion and Resurrection the "second birth" of baptism, the initiatory blow on the cheek at confirmation, the symbolic eating of the Flesh and drinking of the Blood) solemnly and sometimes effectively we are united to those immortal images of initiatory might . . . which man, since the beginning of his day on earth has dispelled the terrors of phenomenality and won through to the all-transfiguring vision of immortal being."

an everlasting afterlife, a resurrection. This is the urge that we satisfy when we worship.

SUMMARY: HAZARD WARNING— "THIS PRODUCT IS ONLY TO BE TAKEN INTERNALLY, NOT LITERALLY"

If we put all of this together, what do we get? It is quite clear that as a species, we have consistently demonstrated a deep urge to believe, and also that in the communication of abstract concepts among human beings, myths and legends have always been important and powerful instruments. To put it simply: we all believe, and we all mythologize. We communicate our most difficult and abstract concepts in story form to each other, and we use the myth format often, particularly when we are talking about deep-seated abstract concepts such as our beliefs. Those beliefs, and their attendant legends, may centre on historical figures, legendary heroes or gods, and in many cultures there is clearly a continuum with overlap and blending of the three. Myths and legends serve specific and important functions in the way human minds work, and (probably) it will always be that way. That's not the problem.

The problems for humankind begin when myths are taken literally. In fact, one might go so far as to say that if myths and legends were not taken so literally, there would be far less trouble in the world.

Troubles start when one group of people takes its own myths, legends and beliefs too literally and uses them to justify conquering or killing people of different beliefs. Worse still, they project their unconscious desires and ambitions into myth form and so create a legend that justifies their own desires. This aspect of myth was brilliantly analyzed by Campbell and by those who influenced him, especially Carl Jung. His writings make the important point that while myths may be interpreted as expressions of the subconscious, the opposite is also true. As Campbell put it, "Mythology . . . is psychology misread as biography, history and cosmogony." When we put somebody or something onto the mythic pedestal—however enjoyable and rewarding that activity is for us—the choice of what we put there and the ways we regard it may be more a reflection of ourselves than of the object of our worship. Myths work best as myths; they cause trouble when they are taken as literal truths.

Campbell understood the social role and the symbolic power of myths and legends within a community better than anyone else. Their value and potency are so great that they genuinely cannot be overstated. Myths and legends (among their many functions) serve as outward and publicly acceptable manifestations within a community of the inner thoughts and desires of its members. They can be ways for us all to express our longings—for many things, including the promise of rescue and redemption. They are the social projections of our inner dreams and aspirations. When we carry out a public act of worship based on a shared belief, we can gather together and in unison express our inner desires. A communal act of belief is a way of making us feel better, and also of exemplifying and clarifying those things that we believe are good.

But that is just one feature or facet of the role of mythology in human consciousness. Perhaps the best and most definitive summary of the many facets of mythology is expressed by Campbell when he writes:

> Mythology has been interpreted by the modern intellect as a primitive fumbling effort to explain the world of nature (Frazer); as a production of poetical fantasy from prehistoric times, misunderstood by succeeding ages (Muller); as a repository of allegorical instruction, to shape the individual to his group (Durkheim); as a group dream, symptomatic of archetypal urges within the depths of the human psyche (Jung); as the traditional vehicle of man's profoundest metaphysical

> insights (Coomaramswamy); and as God's Revelation to His children (the Church). Mythology is all of these.

I cannot imagine a better way of expressing the central roles of our myths than that: "mythology is all of these."

So now we have an understanding of some of the forces that spur us towards belief, and to take myths and legends as the most powerful methods of transmitting those ideas. Let us now move on to look at what beliefs do for the individual who holds them—the psychological and personal benefits that beliefs bring.

CHAPTER THREE

Function and Value: What Belief Does for the Believer

COPING STRATEGIES AND THE NEED TO BELIEVE

In this chapter I shall move along a path brilliantly explored by William James. James was one of the first to analyze the role of religion in the workings of the human mind. He examined religion—relatively dispassionately—and asked questions about what religious beliefs did for the community where they were practised. Although my starting point is very different from his (he clearly had very strong personal theist beliefs), I shall describe some of the inferences that we can make about the role of religion in our times and what function it serves in forming our attitudes and behaviour.

James was genuinely a pioneer in the study of the role of religion in human psychology. He worked—with enormous insight and considerable predictive ability—using the full extent of knowledge and understanding about the human mind that was available in the early twentieth century. In 1902 he published what most people think of as his most important work, *The Varieties of Religious Experience: A Study in Human Nature*. Today, a century later, we have more information to work with. We have many more facts, much more research, many more and newer theories and—just as important—we have a wider vocabulary with which to describe and integrate our concepts of the mind and of religion. So it is now possible to go some distance further than James did in trying to answer the central question, What does religious belief do for the believer? (By the way, in this chapter we shall discuss the benefits of belief to the *individual*; in Chapter 5 we will look at what belief does for a *community* and for the organization and function of groups of people.)

Clearly, the act of believing is a central component of the mechanism by which humankind perceives and responds to the world—and that's because it is so useful. It has value. The act of believing is helpful to us, it works for us, and that beneficial function is a phenomenon in itself. The fact that a belief is valuable to millions of people doesn't necessarily mean that the object at the centre of the belief is proven to exist (as a real entity), but it does mean that the *effect* of the belief is real. It is almost tangible. You can see that effect in the *behaviour* of those who hold that belief. A belief that works is a valid occurrence and phenomenon of itself.

In words used by psychiatrists, the act of thinking about a problem in a beneficial way that reduces its traumatic effect is called a "coping strategy." It is a form of support that assists in functioning when we are threatened by an event and when we feel we are about to be overwhelmed.

I suggest that believing in an external deity performs the function of a coping strategy in the human psyche. It helps the people who do believe in an external deity (which is the majority) to cope with the world. Of course, I am not saying that belief has no other function than this (I shall discuss inspiration, motivation and other similar functions in Chapter 6), but it is very useful to think about belief in this way, as a coping strategy—an activity that helps humankind.

What is true for humankind as a whole is also true for the individual. A coping strategy is a set of insights, perceptions, thoughts and feelings that go on inside someone's mind—it is a personal experience. And that is how some religions (but not all) perceive all religious activity, and not just prayer. Some religions do not regard god as an external intelligence with its own mind and will; instead, they regard god entirely as a person's state of mind. They call that state a transcendent state, in which the individual thinks and behaves differently from his or her ordinary, everyday responses to the world. They regard the act of approaching their god as a progressive change in the state of mind of the person—something that can be achieved inside that individual's mind and soul by altering her or his way of thinking and behaving. They would not regard the simple act of going to a designated building and saying certain scripted words as a guaranteed method of achieving transcendence.

To me, the central point here is almost unarguable: belief in an external deity has a crucial place in the ability of our species to cope with the world. It is difficult to imagine how we would have coped so far without it. To a phrase often attributed to Voltaire, "If God didn't exist, man would have to have invented Him," I would like to add a simple supplementary statement: *even if god does not exist, man's belief in god does*. And it has often been of great help.

"IT'S ALL PART OF THE DIVINE PLAN": COPING WITH DISASTER

Dreadful things happen. There is no doubt about that. There are catastrophes on the individual scale, on the community scale, on the national scale and on the multinational scale (such as the Black Death). Some of the catastrophes are geological, such as earthquakes and floods; some are man-made, such as wars and acts of genocide; and some are biological, such as plagues and epidemics.

In all cases, it seems that humans who witness or are caught up in a catastrophe immediately search for a *reason* for what has just happened. I first realized the almost inescapable power of this need to believe when I was about twelve and I read a front-page newspaper story about a disaster at a skating rink during an ice show for children. The story horrified me, and at the same time I distinctly remember understanding something important about how the survivors coped with catastrophe.

Hundreds of kids were sitting with their parents watching the show at the arena, when a gas furnace situated under the seating area suddenly exploded. The explosion was so massive that many children were killed instantly, many more injured, and many bodies were thrown onto the ice by the blast. According to the newspaper story, some parents—themselves injured—were seen holding the bodies of their children, totally distraught, saying, "It's part of the show—it *has* to be."

I have never forgotten that story. The significance of what those poor parents said was immediately apparent:

in the face of overwhelming tragedy, we all look for some meaning. Those parents needed—for that instant, at least—to believe that the catastrophe that had just occurred was part of some overall plan, however unlikely or incomprehensible that was, while of course part of their minds was telling them the exact opposite. (I have always thought, by the way, that I would react in exactly the same way in a catastrophe like that, and that I would certainly cling for a moment to that same desperate belief if it were my child who had been killed.) That reflex action to believe even for a moment that a catastrophe is actually part of a design is, clearly, an extremely deep and powerful human urge. It is part of the way our minds cope (at least temporarily) with a tragedy so vast that it would otherwise swamp us totally.

The demonstration of that deep-seated need, in my view, explains why humans are so ready to believe in an external deity and a divine design for the universe. It is the same urge at work—to feel that whatever happens, however grim and however awful, is at least part of a grand scheme of things. That belief cannot of course reverse the catastrophe or disaster, but it can assuage the despair and give a sense of meaning to what is otherwise a meaningless tragedy.

The apparent randomness of the disaster is an important feature. When the victim cannot discern any purpose in the accident, and there is no obvious cause or source to blame, the reflex that I am talking about (belief in an overall design or plan) is often activated. Further evidence of this comes from a simple phrase that we are all accustomed to. It is no coincidence that insurance companies have called earthquakes and floods "Acts of God," by which they mean that these events are beyond human prediction and protection (and—far more important—are beyond insurance payouts, unless you take out a special policy with a huge premium). The phrase shows how we link unpredictable natural catastrophes to the implied overall plan of the Creator.

But the phrase "Act of God" also embodies another kind of thought, one that influences the way that survivors of a disaster think and talk about it. If a person survives a disaster that has caused the death of others, it is very common for the survivor to feel that he or she has been selected or chosen—that there is some reason or meaning attached to this particular person's survival and life, that it is part of a grand design.

We have all read stories like that. For example, in September 1999 there was a horrendous traffic accident involving about eighty vehicles on a highway near Windsor, Ontario. A great deal of fuel was spilled and several vehicles caught fire, resulting in the deaths of seven people. Among the survivors, one woman said that

God had been looking after her in there. "God was with me," she said. "He had to be." The interview with this survivor was shown on every television news report and repeated in the press the following day. In the same story it was reported that a fourteen-year-old girl had died in that same accident, and that people had tried to rescue her but were beaten back by the flames. She had cried out to them, "Help me, I'm only fourteen!"

The inconsistency in our attitudes leaps out from that story. Like all of us, I was very glad that the middle-aged woman survived, and was deeply (and I mean deeply) saddened by the tragic death of the young girl. But why call in the *force majeur* of a deity? Did the survivor genuinely mean that there was a God who looked over that accident and chose to preserve the life of the woman and to end the life of the girl? I doubt it. It is highly unlikely that if the survivor had been asked the question directly she would have said, "Yes, I am sure that God intended that poor young girl to die." Of course she would not have said that—yet that is the inescapable implication of the story.

There are two ways of seeing this kind of selectivity in catastrophes. One way is to accept that there genuinely is a divine plan and that, yes, God did intend the young girl to die, and that we humans are unworthy to understand the final and perfect objective of that plan.

Even so, according to this view, we must simply trust the workings of the divinity. The overall design is inscrutable, inaccessible, mysterious, totally occult or perhaps revealed to a very few, but nevertheless, true believers do (and must) believe in it.

The opposing view is just as simple and intelligible. It is this: the survivor's claim of divine protection is no more than—and no less than—a perfectly normal reaction to horror. It is socially acceptable (which is why stories like these are on the news all the time) and it is a natural, innate coping strategy that we all use in the face of overwhelming catastrophe. It gives us all, when we survive a tragedy, a sense of meaning. That sense of meaning is not an actual reality, but it is a way that we can look at the catastrophe and lessen its devastating effect on us.

That social mechanism is so normal and so common that one very rarely hears or reads anything different. I know of only one event in which a survivor had the courage to stress the arbitrary and random nature of the tragedy. It happened in Australia at a skiing resort in the mountains, where an unsuspected and undetected flow of water from a thaw had loosened part of a mountain. A sudden mudslide swept down and obliterated a hotel, killing more than a dozen people. Rescuers did not expect to find any survivors in the part of the hotel that was crushed, but after two days they heard noises. They located and managed to rescue a man named Stewart Driver, whose young wife had been killed in the accident. He attributed his survival purely to the laws of physics—it *just happened* that the part of the hotel that collapsed didn't fall in such a way as to kill him. In my view, his remark shows a fortitude and courage of exceptional depth. To survive physically in those circumstances is in itself remarkable, to lose your wife in the same accident is tragic, but to be able to call upon that personal resource and to maintain a genuinely philosophical attitude is absolutely astonishing.

Please do not misunderstand me. I am not saying that the woman in the highway accident was "wrong" or that Stewart Driver was "right." That is not the point at all. The point is that when confronted with a disaster, most people seek an explanation that involves a plan or design for the universe—only a few people such as Stewart Driver can face arbitrary events without taking that sort of *refuge*. The really significant difference between the two incidents is the intellectual fortitude and courage shown by the person who saw the tragedy unfold.

"IT'LL ALL BE BETTER IN THE END": COPING WITH MAN-MADE PRIVATION AND SUFFERING

We have been looking at accidents with no obvious cause or source—events that are, as far as we can tell, totally random. In such cases there is generally no obvious focus of blame. Yet even when there is a clearly human cause of the misery, the concept of a divine plan may still allow the sufferers to take comfort: a belief system may still (and often does) act as a genuine coping strategy. People have always looked to their concept of a god to help them in times of suffering, even when that suffering is caused not by divine (or random) intervention but by human agency.

Belief in god was a source of comfort to victims of religious persecution (from the Crusades through the Inquisition to the Holocaust). It was important to the victims of the slave traffic from Africa to America, and in countless examples of mass torture, persecution, imprisonment, execution and other acts of cruelty and destruction perpetrated by one group of humans against another. Belief has always been one of the most important forms of support.

There is no wrong or right about this. It is simply and clearly one of the benefits that belief brings to the believer: he or she can take comfort in that belief in the face of vicissitudes. When disaster strikes, even though the disaster is clearly caused by human agency, the victims of that disaster can still gain comfort and support from a belief in a deity. That belief often strengthens and is more valuable in the face of catastrophe and suffering than it is at other times. It is simply one of the ways that belief works as a part of the human psyche.

"NOTHING MAKES SENSE OTHERWISE": COPING WITH THE UNKNOWN

A few years ago, while I was filming a sequence for a TV series in California, I got into a round-table debate with a woman from San Diego. She became very vehement about the existence of God, and at one point she said (*very* firmly), "Of course God exists. It's the only way to make sense of everything. If God didn't exist, I can't understand how the universe could work!"

At that point the debate degenerated somewhat. I suggested that she might not understand how a telephone works (she said she didn't), but the mere fact of a person being mystified by a telephone is not proof that God exists, any more than her being mystified by the universe is. I am mystified by the universe too—but, like most non-theists, I acknowledge the fact that my mystification might say more about the limitations of my brain than it says about a divine creator.

That woman's argument, though, is often used as a proof of theism: if scientists cannot explain the workings of the cosmos, this is proof that God exists, because only he can know it all.

Like so many theological issues, this is a debate that

cannot be resolved by factual data. Those with a theist belief assert that the entire mysterious cosmos is the creation of an intelligence so much greater than our own that we cannot comprehend its magnitude or its plan. The opposing view is this: whether there is such an intelligence or not, there is clearly a human predilection for dealing with the unknown by labelling it "god," which allows us to feel that we know it (or partly know it). The evidence supporting this assertion, say the non-theists, includes the observation that humans are clearly more comfortable grappling with the unknown when it bears a familiar label and we can then ascribe certain properties to it. It is one way the human mind works. To put the sequence of events in order, it goes like this: having personified that unknown-ness, those who believe in that external god may now imagine that it/he/she, in return, knows them. The believers are in effect saying: "We believe in a something that watches over us and we believe that that particular something has a special reason for looking after us. Or at least for looking after those of us who have a personal relationship with it—as opposed to those others, the unbelievers, who merely and mistakenly regard the unknown as 'the unknown.'"

As has been said often, the concept of god is wonderfully comforting when you find yourself in a threatening and mysterious place: there was a saying during the First World War that there are no atheists in foxholes. We all tend to call out familiar names in the dark.

PROMISES, PROMISES

FUTURE JOY: THE GOLD AT THE END OF THE RAINBOW

Some authorities in the past have compared religious faith to buying an insurance policy with the premiums paid by regular acts of devotion and observance, and the policy promises a large and totally intangible payout after the insured person has died.

It may well be that as the old saying has it, the promises of eternal salvation and life offered by religion are no more than a promise of "pie in the sky when you die." This aspect of belief in an external deity is extremely important. What I have been talking about is the function of religious belief as a coping strategy, supporting the believer in facing various aspects of the world, but the "promises" aspect is totally different. The allures and promises ostensibly made by external deities are multi-faceted.

"THE ROAD MAP TO HEAVEN": THE ALLURE OF INFALLIBLE RULES

While I was making a television series in West Virginia, the TV crew and I visited a strange sect of Christians in a very small, impoverished town called Jolo. At the Sunday church services, the preachers and worshippers would dance holding live rattlesnakes and copperheads in their hands. They believed that dancing with potentially lethal snakes was a test of their faith. There are two verses from the Gospel According to St. Mark (16:17, 18) that can be interpreted (at a stretch) as a promise of immunity from harm, although they were almost certainly meant as a statement about the metaphorical power of faith to overcome adversity: "And these signs shall follow them that believe; in my name shall they cast out devils; they shall speak with new tongues; they shall take up serpents; and if they drink any deadly thing, it shall not hurt them . . ."

As part of their service, as a sort of work-up to the snake dance, the preacher got more and more frenetic (as did the congregation), asking worshippers to put all their faith in the Lord. At one point he waved the Bible above his head, then brandished it at the congregation and yelled, "This is the only book you'll ever need! It's got everything in it, right here! This book is a road map to the Kingdom of Heaven!" His message and his emotion were quite sincere—he really meant just that, and the congregation agreed.

Many people genuinely believe that if they do everything the Bible says, their place in heaven is guaranteed.

The Bible offers them the complete book of the rules of life—every question answered, all paths and options mapped out for them. It's the only book they'll ever need.

This allure of the road map offered by a strong theist belief is enormously attractive, because basically life is perplexing, and everyone wants clear and comprehensible answers. We all hanker after a set of clear and unequivocal rules and guidelines that we can obey and that will solve all the problems and conflicts and ambiguities of real life. It is (in some ways) a very attractive prospect—no more decisions, no more dilemmas, just a pure and simple Code of Behaviour. Perhaps the neatest phrasing of the pure-and-sublime-orderliness lifestyle came in T. H. White's novel *The Once and Future King*. The young lad who will be King Arthur has several magical metamorphoses (performed by Merlin) in which he tries out the lifestyles of various animals. When he becomes an ant, he experiences as a member of a large ant colony the extremes of order, regulation and robotic obedience. The cornerstone maxim of the ants is expressed in a simple statement of pure and blind obedience: "EVERYTHING THAT IS NOT FORBIDDEN IS COMPULSORY." That is perhaps an extreme example of the desire to have rules and regulations covering every aspect of existence, but I suspect that there are people on this planet who would quite welcome it.

THE ALLURE OF IMMORTALITY

As the old saying goes, "Nobody gets out of life alive."

Of course we all know that fact (the other old saying about nothing being certain except death and taxes belabours the point). Nevertheless, the knowledge of our own mortality is extremely uncomfortable. It might be regarded, in our more philosophical moments, as an unpleasant but inescapable feature of human consciousness. Probably shortly after our species developed a sense of awareness of ourselves and of the world around us, we realized that life is circumscribed. Every human life—no matter how worthwhile, exalted, productive, creative, philanthropic or brilliant—ends in death. A medical ethicist put it well when he remarked that "despite all the miracles and breakthroughs of modern medicine, the death rate will always remain exactly the same—precisely one death per person."

So, we human beings bear an awareness of our own mortality (although it is quite possible that we are not the only species on earth that is so endowed—some zoologists suggest that elephants mulling over their forbears' bones might be aware of the reality of those deaths). But whether we are the exclusive owners of this knowledge or not, we don't like it. The inevitability of our own death is never a pleasant subject to contemplate.

As it turns out, the great majority of humankind over the last few millennia have found the knowledge of mortality basically unacceptable, and have always quested for something more than—and something more permanent than—this excessively brief lifespan.

So, I contend, it is possible that humans invented the concept of immortality to help them deal with the dread of dying. And, as we can all see, it works. There is no doubt that it is comforting to think of a continuity between the living and the dead that survives and transcends death. The thought of being united with children, relatives and loved ones after death makes the prospect of death obviously less dreaded and awful. The thought that one might "carry on" in some form or other, using one's mind or some other aspect of one's personality in some way, is genuinely reassuring.

Of course, nobody actually knows whether there is a life after death. Those who believe in it say that it has been affirmed in the Bible (or the holy book of their religion), that stories of people ascending to heaven are legion, and that stories of people seeing visions of the deceased are so frequent that they number many millions. And, the argument goes, so many millions of people cannot be wrong.

The opposing argument does not deny any of these statements. Those who do not believe in an afterlife simply observe that the desire for immortality is an unfathomably deep urge—so deep and powerful and primal that it can best be considered as a basic component of the human psyche. As such, it is not surprising that most humans believe it. To believe in an afterlife, the non-believers say, is so basic an instinct that the billions who believe it are not proving that they are right, they are merely proving that they are human.

This is not a debate that can be settled by factual data. Stories of people claiming to return after death having met relatives and friends in the afterlife can never (in the current state of knowledge) be proven and substantiated. They cannot be proven as facts demonstrable to an objective third party in the same way that, say, the presence of oil underground, or the height of Mount Everest, or the existence of the pi-meson atomic particle can be proven. In fact (as we will discuss in Chapter 4), even the feeling that one has had an experience of an afterlife, complete with visions of a white light and perhaps feelings of meeting others, can be produced by stimulation of a certain part of the brain. So, the non-believers maintain, it might not be the brain seeing something (an afterlife) that actually exists, it might be the way the brain responds physiologically to certain types of near-disaster.

To some extent, whether or not an afterlife actually exists, or in what way it exists, is not the point—and it is certainly beyond the scope of this book. The important point is that the concept of an afterlife—just like the concept of a god—serves several important functions in helping humans cope with the world, and in coping with the fact of death in particular.

What I am saying is that being aware of our own mortality is an awkward but inevitable side effect of having acquired consciousness. It is undoubtedly an unfair trick of nature to saddle conscious, sentient beings with this deep insult to our intellect—the knowledge that our own lives are brief and will end—but it's the way evolution has turned out. And, seen in the context of the different forms of life on this planet, it might still be preferable to possess consciousness and to suffer the discomfort of the knowledge of mortality than to exist like a bump on a log with no consciousness at all.

The Danish philosopher Søren Kierkegaard proposed that the awareness and fear of dying is so fundamental to human nature that it underlies most human beliefs and ways of behaving. If he is right, and if the many observers of the functions of religion are right too, then there is a lot to be gained from a belief in an afterlife. Perhaps—to paraphrase a common saying—the reward is not a guarantee of life eternal, but at least a way of dealing with the fear of death.

JUDGMENT DAY: THE ALLURE OF PERFECT JUSTICE

Another value of belief in a deity is the concept of ultimate justice—that somewhere there is a being that can discern the genuinely Right from the genuinely Wrong and who will mete out reward and punishment appropriately.

In Greek theatre in ancient times (we're talking about Sophocles and the pre-Christian playwrights here), human tragedies and catastrophes were often resolved by an innovative theatrical device. What happened was that in the final act, a deity figure was lowered by a stage machine (a sort of crane) into the play, and the deity pronounced from his/her/its chariot/throne/device the solution to all the problems. Whereupon the mortals marvelled, the characters in the play all accepted the divine dicta, and the theatre-goers all went home happy.

That dramatic convention was called, in later Latin translation, the *deus ex machina* ("the god from the machine"). It made sense to the ancient Greek theatrical audiences and (to some extent) it makes sense now. Evidence for its satisfying appeal can be found in a vast number of novels, fables and of course that definer of world culture, Hollywood movies.

The important point here is the communality of human experience—the *deus ex machina*, angels, Satan and so on are all immediately intelligible to us because they all spring from the same system of human thinking. They are all signs (or symptoms, if you like) of the way we prefer to think about the world. We like—and instinctively move towards—salvation figures that sort out the good (which they reward) from the bad (which is punished). We like to think about things that way; it was popular back then, and it's still popular today.

This is not surprising. Clearly, we all share an urge to see our problems sorted out by a force or being greater than ourselves. It is quite likely that the *deus ex machina* was the antecedent of the medieval view of Judgment Day and of the souls of the dead being assigned to Heaven or Hell depending on the quality of their life on earth. Furthermore, it is equally likely that the divine verdicts spoken by the *deus* from his (or perhaps her) *machina* would reflect the values of that society at that particular time. The same is true of the tales told of Judgment Day. The justice envisioned might be described as perfect, but the exact vision of perfection is always defined in the terms of contemporary social values, and usually includes the visionary's view of Perfect Revenge on his enemies. A good example of this, by the way, is Dante's *Inferno*. Dante was quite the political animal and incurred the wrath of several big-time politicos, who had him exiled. Accordingly, some of his enemies appear in his *Inferno*, where they turn up in some of the more pernicious circles of Hell suffering all kinds of nasty and extreme punishment. If one took *Inferno* literally, one would have to think that Satan was closely following the agenda of that very serious gentleman Dante Alighieri.

But—to be less frivolous about this issue—the desire for something outside ourselves that will sort out all of our problems is a major feature of most religious systems. Whether it contains ingredients of revenge and score settling or not, the vision of Perfect Justice is clearly an important part of the function of religious belief for many believers.

"STARLIGHT, STAR BRIGHT": THE ALLURE OF WISH-FULFILLMENT

As the old joke has it, the person who wants more and gets it has only one remaining desire from that moment on—to get *more* more.

Every single one of us has a wish list. There is nobody who could, in all honesty, answer the question, "What do you really wish for?" with a shrug and "Nothing, I've got it all. Thanks for asking."

The relationship between concepts of god and wish-fulfillment has always been close. In fact, the desire to have one's wishes granted is the direct descendant of intercessionary prayer (as we discussed in Chapter 1).

There is no difference in format between someone asking for their wishes to be fulfilled at, for example, the TV evangelical meetings seen every Sunday and the ancient "We give you food, now give us turtles" mentioned by Frazer in *The Golden Bough*. Perhaps this material and "gimme" aspect of some prayer is best satirized in the famous Janis Joplin song "Oh Lord, won't you buy me a Mercedes-Benz!"

At a more general and more serious level, wish-fulfillment extends beyond the immediate desire for a new car or a round of drinks. Underlying the immediate and material yearnings are more deep-seated desires for an omnipotent and benign ultimate guardian. Perhaps—as has been said before—the ultimate wish is for salvation. Perhaps what we all long for is Someone—a power greater than we can understand—to rescue us, to sort out our problems and to reward our essential goodness with wish-fulfillment.

When you start thinking about the wish-fulfillment aspect of human belief, it is easy to see common themes running through all kinds of myths and legends. Perhaps the most obvious example is in the Santa Claus fable. The concept of Santa Claus contains many of the central elements: reward for the people (children) who have behaved well, lack of reward (a lump of coal) for those who have not, magical powers in the awarding of the gifts (visiting all children in one night) and so on. The fact that there might possibly have been a genuine Niklaus who made anonymous donations to some impoverished women by dropping money down their chimneys, and that he might have been canonized because of that, adds to the blurring of the dividing line between myth and religion.

Clearly, invoking supernatural powers of any description is given additional momentum by the very human desire to have our wishes fulfilled. But there is more to the act of praying than simply hoping that a Saint Niklaus will drop coins down your chimney—the action of framing a prayer has psychological effects of its own. Let's discuss those now.

PRAYER: PROCESS AND OUTCOME

Prayer helps. We all know that.

As a physician I see it all the time when patients tell me about what they experience when they pray. You do not need to be a theist or to have a belief in any religion to see the benefit that comes from the act of praying. The benefit comes to the person who prays *whether the request in the prayer is granted or not*. With prayer—as with so many important human actions—there is a difference between process and outcome. The process of praying is a state of mind that the person enters into: when it works, it produces some measure of tranquility, of resolution and a feeling of making contact with inner resource and strength. That action—the process—happens whether what is being asked for is granted or not.

A chaplain at our hospital put it beautifully when he said that praying is like going to your mother when you are a child and you have grazed your knee. You do not expect that your mother will be able to heal your knee, but the act of going to your mother makes it easier for you to bear the pain—it gives comfort—and so, in a very genuine sense, the pain becomes less.

This difference—between process and outcome—is not trivial. In fact, many religions do not seem to be particularly interested in outcome at all, but regard the entire purpose of a religious activity solely as a process. Many religions have, as a central tenet of their belief system, the idea that the purpose of prayer is to change the state of mind of the person who is praying. The person makes the prayer in order to achieve peace or some transcendent state (even a trance, if need be). The use of repetitive words, chants or mantras is simply a mechanism to induce in the person a state of calm and contact (many sects of Buddhism are prime examples of this). In some religions it would be regarded as quite peculiar to go into a big hall with other people and to ask for things without first doing or saying something of personal significance to ensure that one is in the appropriate psychological state. They would regard incessant inter-church arguments about details of services, observances and interpretations as bizarre, and entirely contrary to the original idea of contact with god.[1]

Prayer—seen as an action of the human mind—is similar to the child's seeking solace from a parent after an injury. The action changes the state of the person's mind, and changes the meaning of what is happening to that person, but not necessarily the injury itself. Whether you believe in god or not, the act of prayer is clearly of therapeutic benefit for most of humankind. As the quotation from William James at the front of this book puts it so well, beliefs do not work because they are true, but are true because they work.

1. These differences in observances and ceremony are really rather superficial. As Michael Schulman neatly puts it, "The different religions of the world do not show, as many insist, that all people worship the same god in different ways. Instead, humans worship *different* gods in the *same* ways. The world's varied gods present us with very different 'personalities' and precepts, and each religion has its own unique and *mutually exclusive* creation myth, pantheon of supernatural entities, and vision of life after death. But the *ways* of worship are essentially the same: rituals, prayers, chants, acts of offering or self-denial, special gestures before revered objects or images, all led by special people wearing special costumes or adornments, in special places and at special times."

INCIDENTAL BENEFITS OF RELIGIOUS EXPERIENCE

There are, of course, many other benefits that accrue from religious and spiritual beliefs, and some of these are sometimes taken as factual proof of the existence of god or of a supernatural intelligence.

I would like to propose that these undoubted benefits are not proof of any extra-human forces, but—in addition to being wonderful—simply illustrate how little we understand of human creativity. To put it simply: the ceiling of the Sistine Chapel is absolutely astounding and it shows what humans are capable of—but it is not in itself proof of the existence of god or angels or Adam and Eve.

INSPIRATION: GOD HAS THE BEST TUNES

To a lot of people it is obvious that some acts of creativity (usually in the arts but sometimes in other disciplines) are so astonishing and so far beyond normal human capabilities that they can only have originated from a divine source. The ceiling of the Sistine Chapel—so the argument goes—is so magnificent and a work of such inspired genius that it cannot be the work of a human alone; it must prove that a divinity exists.

Of course—as with many of the issues that I have

discussed so far in this book—there can be no absolute proof or disproof of this notion. However, it has often been said (and there is more than a grain of truth in it) that god has all the best tunes (and, one might add, some of the best paintings, sculptures and literature).

Those who have strong theist beliefs might feel that the acts of creativity that emanate from artists when inspired by god are so far beyond the realm of ordinary human talent that they are proof of an external source of energy—an inspiration. The flaw in the logic here is simply that we have no real idea what the limits of human creativity are. To label an extraordinary act of genius "divine" is no more than saying "I don't know how he did that." People in the fourteenth century said it of Dante, in the seventeenth century of Shakespeare, and then of Mozart and Einstein and now of Stephen Hawking. The fact that we don't know where the ideas and visions come from doesn't prove that they are of extra-human origin, but it does say something about our recognition of our own limitations.

The non-theist view is that humankind is a biological population, and that in any biological populations there are a few people at either end of the spectrum. While most of us are bunched fairly closely together in the "average" group, there are always the outlying individuals. In any population there are always, by definition, a few people at the edges of the bell curve—people who are very tall, very short, very heavy, very light, very intelligent, very stupid, very creative or very uncreative. You might only get one Michelangelo every few centuries, but that's a simple statement of statistics.

Furthermore, this view goes, people can excel and be seen as geniuses only within the context of the creative activities of their times. Michelangelo painted the Sistine Chapel ceiling with images of angels, god, Adam and so on because that is what the times demanded. He was commissioned by the Pope, who wanted something that would astonish the people. Michelangelo was a genius and he painted—in his genius way—what people expected a painting to look like, only much, much better. But it was still dictated by the mores of the times. If Michelangelo had had a vision of what van Gogh would be painting a few centuries later and had done the Sistine Chapel ceiling in a repeating pattern of sunflowers, for example, the Pope wouldn't have given him any more work. As Gore Vidal once said in an interview, Michelangelo was basically a closet Hellenist (i.e., a pagan) who used his genius to paint divine and religious subjects because that was what the market demanded at the time.

So, the fact that images of god and theist themes have been the focus or content of so many works of art is simply a statement of the way geniuses express their extraordinary talents. It is not necessarily proof of an external source for the inspiration. The content is dictated by the times the artist lives in; the genius is the artist's genius; and biology predicts that there will always be geniuses.

BEAUTY, LOVE AND OTHER ATTRIBUTES OF THE SOUL

Another argument often used in support of theist beliefs is that non-theists must be very peculiar people (well, weird, actually) because they must be ruled solely by reason and therefore lack any emotion, soul, spirituality, love or sensitivity. If you don't believe in anything beyond the human race, this argument goes, then you can't have any sense of the finer things—you must be soulless.

The opposing view is simple: there is no connection between religious views, on the one hand, and the understanding and experience of human emotions, on the other. They may both be very important in the makeup of an individual, but they have nothing to do with each other. Supporting evidence is close at hand; this is a simple matter of everyday observation. We all know people who have deep religious beliefs but who, in general, are extremely unemotional, are frequently insensitive to their own feelings and those of others (I call that being "emotionally colour-blind") and have great or even insuperable difficulty in discussing matters of the heart.

But we all know examples of the opposite. There are quite a few good-hearted and sensitive non-theists (I've met a lot of them, so I know what I'm talking about) who have no difficulty understanding and experiencing love, doubt, artistic genius, natural wonder, awe and (I use the word rarely!) ecstasy.

A sense of beauty, love, awe for nature and for great art are not the exclusive properties of theists. Being sensitive to and appreciative of the world around you is not related to issues of religious belief. People who do not have insight into their own emotions are quite likely to be destructive and often will be insensitive to the emotions of others. The major point here is simple (and not very controversial). Even though, throughout history, many artistic and inspirational achievements have been linked with a belief in an external deity, it is not true that you *have* to hold such a belief in order to experience the same emotions and (if your talents lie in that direction) create works of artistic merit.

The disproof of the "non-theists are emotionless robots" idea can exist only at a personal level. If you know a few people who are non-theists but who clearly do possess an understanding of human emotion (theirs and others) and of beauty, awe and all the other important sensitivities, you know that the "emotionless robots" idea is fallacious.

"BLESS YOU!": SOCIAL FUNCTION SUPERIMPOSED ON BELIEF

So far, then, we have been discussing the function of belief in terms of coping—coping with disasters, coping with deprivation and suffering and coping with the fear of death. However, after beliefs have been shared by a large number of people, social customs based on a belief acquire a life and a value of their own.

For example, think of the phrase "Bless you!"

All of us are accustomed to the idea of saying "Bless you!" when somebody sneezes. Originally (so it is said) this custom grew up from a belief in the Middle Ages that while a person sneezes they are temporarily vulnerable to possession by a demon or devil. So, to prevent the demon from taking advantage of the moment and sneaking into the sneezer's body at a weak moment, a friend says, "God bless you!" (now usually contracted to "Bless you!"). At the sound of this (one assumes), the demon realizes that the advantage has been lost, shrugs and mutters, "Some other time, perhaps," to itself and slinks off back to Hades.

Most of the people who say "Bless you!" probably have no idea of the origin of the custom. Presumably in the Middle Ages it was regarded as an act of great altruism and importance; now it is merely a symbolic phrase, indicating the politeness of the blesser and a socialized concern for the blessee. But—and this is the point about all interpersonal acts that have acquired their own significance—it now functions as an audible expression of goodwill, a once-significant custom now overlaid with a mild social graciousness.

The same is true of any form of belief, whether it was originally religious or not: it can acquire a social function of its own. Even superstitions such as throwing salt over your shoulder if you spill some at the table can become a simple social custom or grace. The important point is that the custom that evolves from a belief acquires its own function and value—and the truth or validity of the origin of that custom (e.g., salt throwing, saying "Bless you!") need not detract from the validity of the custom itself.

If we all use something as a coping strategy in our social transactions, that custom has value as a social coping strategy. Whether the original idea or belief is true or untrue does not matter—and we shall discuss this further when we look at the social function of religious ceremonies and institutions in Chapter 6.

WHAT DO PEOPLE *REALLY* BELIEVE IN?

So far we have been talking about belief—its origins, its functions and its values—as if it were a single capability of the human mind, a switch that is either in the "on" (belief) position or the "off" (disbelief) position.

In real life, belief is not like that. (Or so I believe!)

When you think about it, there are several quite distinct levels of belief, and we all may believe (or disbelieve) various things at different intensities or to different degrees or at different levels or depths.

For example, here is one possible classification, which divides the activity of believing into six categories:

1. **Complete or total belief:** A belief held totally and unshakably. The belief is a central part of the person's outlook on the world, so that a change in that belief would produce a change in the personality and the behaviour of that individual. The belief goes "all the way down" and is maintained by the person despite any lack of factual data or in the face of any contradictory data. Most religious and spiritual beliefs are of this type and degree and many religious people would describe their own personal belief in their god as complete and total.

2. Partial or potential belief: A belief that a person is ready to hold and capable of holding, but that is not firmly a part of that person's daily life. It is there, but it is not a feature of the individual's normal world-view, and it could be shed or altered without great consequence. Many people, for example, feel that they do partly believe in ghosts or in spirits, or that contact can be made with people who have died. They have moments or experiences when they do believe these things, but at other times they do not hold to that belief firmly. This type of intensity of belief is comparable to an intermittent suspicion or partial conviction.

Many people who would label themselves agnostic—not knowing—about an external god would say that their belief is potential or partial. They do not have complete or total belief, but (if you'll forgive the grammar) they do not *not* believe.

3. Slight and convenient belief: There are many things that large numbers of people believe in to a very slight extent, and only when the outcome is in keeping with their own views and plans. A good example is astrology (others include numerology, palm reading, Tarot cards, and the use of the I Ching in the western world). These are all activities that most people do not take as gospel or as undeniable truth but will note and remember for a while. If events turn out as predicted, a person may well ascribe some magic properties to his or her star sign. On the other hand, most people would not be upset if they had a good day when their horoscope said they would have a bad one. Nor is this type of slight belief challenged when every person born under the sign of Aries does not have the same financial reverses and emotional boosts on the same day.

These kinds of beliefs provide (apart from entertainment and amusement) a socially acceptable and useful rationale for certain types of conflicts (and attractions), as well as a useful method of resolution ("I knew we'd have this fight—Capricorns and Leos always disagree about risk taking.")

4. Beliefs of childhood: Childhood is different. There are many fables and myths that we tell our children and that act as moral guides. Most of them have to do with reward and punishment, and they have always been acceptable methods of explaining to children what is socially acceptable or creditable behaviour and what is not. Figures such as Santa Claus, the Easter Bunny and even the Tooth Fairy are valuable ways of teaching children how to behave well (to "be good all year" or to "be brave about losing that tooth"). Along with these myths, there are very definite social conventions that are deeply held and widely accepted about the appropriateness of these beliefs in different age groups. Adults expect their children to take the belief literally when they are young, but would be surprised if, say, a thirty-year-old man still believed in the Tooth Fairy. Despite movies such as *Miracle on 34th Street*, a sincere belief by an adult in the reality and actual existence of Santa Claus would be regarded as evidence of a mental problem. You might even want to hospitalize for psychiatric support a forty-year-old who kept on shouting that he believed in Santa Claus, but you wouldn't want the same treatment for a five-year-old.

5. Beliefs of small minorities: Some beliefs are held very sincerely by small numbers of people who are not part of the same community. A typical example of this is the belief held by many hundreds of people that they have been abducted by aliens and have had experiments performed on them in alien spaceships. Many of these people have quite marked social difficulties and problems in their own lifestyles (although some do not), and often the alien abduction includes a form of social praise ("You have been selected . . ."). Sometimes the subjects say that they have been subjected to sexual experiments. These beliefs are always deeply held and sometimes reinforced in self-help groups. The individuals who hold these beliefs are accustomed to being called crazy or deluded by people who do not share their beliefs.

Perhaps certain religions that have very small numbers of adherents fit into this category also. For example, the Doukhobors are a small band whose religion includes the practices of nudity and of arson (usually of farm buildings). They are accustomed to both social isolation and having their acts of arson treated as criminal offences.

6. Superstitions: Then there are superstitions. We all have them, but what do we mean by them?

When we throw spilled salt over our left shoulder or walk around a ladder (instead of under it, even if we can see there's nobody on the ladder to drop things on our head), what are we thinking of?

Most people would not connect their own superstitious feelings with any religious experience; they seem to belong to different compartments of the mind. Superstitions are things we go along with "because you never know" or "because there's no sense in taking a chance" or "because I always feel more comfortable when I do" or "because everybody does that—it's normal" or "because it's a habit" or "just because." Nobody would imagine that god would punish them for walking under a ladder, but that trouble might come from "fate" or "destiny" or (if we are being more literary) "the Furies" or simply "the odds."

We all know what we mean by the word "superstition," but at the same time we all know that we don't know in what form the punishment for disobedience will arrive. We know that when we are behaving superstitiously we are trying to propitiate "something out there," but it isn't religion.

This is a difficult type of belief to categorize. In all likelihood the origins of superstitions are in animism—that is, belief in the consciousness of all life and all objects. We know that animism was one of the earliest common beliefs of human societies, and it is very likely that there are remaining vestiges of this deep-seated attitude around (and within) us today. Superstitions would fit the bill very nicely as group instincts derived from animism.

We all draw a clear line between superstition and religion. Even so, from a non-theist point of view, it is possible to see both superstition and religion as manifestations of the same animistic belief system. If you happen to believe that there is no external deity and no external intelligence controlling human affairs, both "casual" superstitions and organized religions are part of the same system of belief.

Does what I have said here make sense to you? Does this idea strike a chord of recognition—do you feel that there are actually different levels of belief and that you might hold one belief with a different intensity or passion or sincerity than you bring to another?

This is a very important point. Currently, we use the word "believe" as if every belief were equivalent in all respects to every other. But if the categorization that I've set out above makes intuitive sense to you, the word "believe" has several different shades of meaning for you. Belief in Santa Claus is not the same kind of belief as belief in Jesus, and it is most unfortunate and confusing that we use the same word to describe, without qualification, all of these different believing activities.

Being aware of the varying degrees of belief may be the first and essential step in avoiding dogmatism and conflict over differences in belief.

THAT WAS THEN, THIS IS NOW

HOW THE UNCHANGEABLE HAS CHANGED

At this point—having discussed the origins and forms of belief in a controlling deity and the many benefits that accrue to the believer—we should pause to consider how the image of god has changed over the course of time. And how that change or evolution in the concept of god reflects the society in which it arises.

There is no doubt that the image, role and definition

of god have changed constantly over the centuries, and it is legitimate to ask why this has happened. Has god himself/herself/itself changed, or is this process simply a matter of the organized religions bowing to the demands and perceptions of the populace? In other words, is this change anything to do with the external deity itself or is it purely a matter of the maturation and development of our own minds and understanding?

A few millennia ago, everyone was content with a figure like the God of Abraham, the protector and guide of a tribe of nomads wandering through the Sinai peninsula. A few thousand years later, we need a concept of a cosmic intelligence that controls the entire universe many billions of light-years across. So is this a matter of human sophistication, or is there an element of divine evolution?

I would like to suggest that in our quest to explain the inexplicable and to find a *because* for every *why*, the concept of god started out as a repository for the things we didn't understand. Over the centuries, however, humankind understood more and more of the previously Unknowable. The Unknowable became a smaller area (even though it's still pretty big) and as it shrank, the number of phenomena that needed the idea of a god to explain them shrank steadily too.

To some extent, the history of the world's religions fits this hypothesis quite well. It's worth looking at a few points in the evolution of religions to cast some light here.

For example, the God of Israel, known by the name Yahweh—the single God of the Jewish and Christian religions—did not emerge without a struggle among other deities. The details are lucidly set out in *A History of God* by Karen Armstrong. She describes how the early Israelites believed that Yahweh/God was one among a council of deities and won out against stiff competition:

> Yahweh did not seem to transcend the older deities in a peaceful natural manner. He had to fight it out. Thus in Psalm Eighty-two we see him making a play for the leadership of the Divine Assembly which had played such an important role in both Babylonian and Canaanite myth:
>
> *Yahweh takes his stand in the Council of El*
> *to deliver judgments among the gods.*
>
> *"No more mockery of justice*
> *no more favouring the wicked!*
> *Let the weak and the orphan have justice,*
> *be fair to the wretched and the destitute,*
> *rescue the weak and needy*
> *save them from the clutches of the wicked."*

I must admit that this came as a complete surprise to me. Before I read Karen Armstrong's book, I had supposed that before belief in one God became widespread, most peoples had simply worshipped several gods. I imagined that the concept of one God won over the other belief systems because the people who believed in one God had gained the upper hand in Palestine. In other words, I had assumed that the religious domination of Yahweh/God was due to the political and geographical domination of the people who happened to believe in him. I had always imagined that if, for example, the followers of Baal had been better equipped, armed and organized than anyone else, Baalism would have become the dominant religion.

What Armstrong describes—in great and fascinating detail—is that the people who believed in Yahweh/God believed that he had won his own political (if I may use that word) victory in the heavens, in the Council of El. Eventually, they believed, it happened that there was only one God because he had shown himself to be the best. The struggle, the victory and dominance, was not between the followers of God and the peoples who believed in other deities, but between Yahweh/God and the other deities themselves. Yahweh/God emerged as the winner not because his followers won, but because *he* won.

This is just one example of the way that the objects of belief—gods—have evolved, according to the legends of their various adherents. It is equally fascinating to read of the evolution of the name Allah, another clear example of the evolution of belief. Here Armstrong summarizes some of the prophet Muhammad's reflections during his retreat to a small cave near the top of Mount Hira during Ramadan in the year 610:

> Like many of the Arabs, Muhammad had come to believe that al-Lah, the High God of the ancient Arabian pantheon whose name simply meant "the God," was identical to the God worshipped by the Jews and the Christians. . . . He also believed that only a prophet of this God could solve the problems of his people, but he never believed for one moment that he was going to be that prophet. Indeed the Arabs were unhappily aware that al-Lah had never sent them a prophet or a scripture of their own, even though they had his shrine in their midst from time immemorial.

THE MATURATION OF EXPLANATION

So, things have changed—what does that tell us?

There are several possible conclusions that can be drawn from the evolution of images of god. One possible conclusion is that human understanding of the deity was initially poor and vague and now has improved and become more sophisticated. God has not changed, but our understanding has.

Supporters of this view frequently point to analogies in other areas, such as our understanding of the brain. Thousands of years ago people did not even believe that the act of thinking went on in the brain. They thought it went on in the heart, and that the brain did nothing but cool the blood. As empirical observations accumulated, this idea was abandoned, but it was accepted as a fact that the brain was populated with spirit forces. Then along came René Descartes. His idea was that the brain was like a system of pipes or conduits conducting vital forces along them. Later, after understanding how electricity works, it became possible to envision brain function as a complex system or network of electrical wires. A few important advances later and we are able to think of the brain as a computer system, with subsystems changing the state of other systems. This allows us to conceptualize a model of how our brains might, for example, recognize patterns or be sensitive to certain kinds of visual stimuli, and so on. The human brain did not change over those centuries, but our ability to explain and describe it did.

Those who believe in the existence of an external deity

feel that the evolution of religious expression is comparable to this process: the phenomenon at the centre has not altered, but the humans observing it have become more adept at conceptualizing it.

The opposite conclusion is equally compelling—that the evolution of religions is a straightforward reflection of the expansion of human knowledge, causing shrinkage of superstition. A few millennia ago, humans did not know anything at all about the universe: they were frightened by it and invented the concept of god or gods to help them face that fear. As more and more became known about the universe, less and less needed to be laid at god's door for explanation. Thus—the argument goes—the shrinkage of the religious realm reflects nothing more than the growth of our factual knowledge.

Of course there is no definitive and correct answer to this, and there can never be one. Theists believe that human understanding of the eternal god has always been incomplete, and that the change in the concept of god is simply due to our own maturation and the increased sophistication of our understanding. Non-theists believe that in its entirety, the concept of god is a human creation reflecting our fear of the unknown (among other things), and, as more of the previously unknown universe is understood, the role of the concept of god shrinks. Since the act of believing is by definition something that extends beyond the range of proven facts and data, this discussion of the unknown can never be factually settled.

Yet even though the *facts* will never be settled, the *psychological* effects and functions of belief can be examined in further detail.

THE NATURAL EVOLUTION OF COPING STRATEGIES

There are ways that this can all be put together.

In many respects, as I said earlier, religious beliefs serve the function of a coping strategy: they assist the possessor to adapt to difficulties, stresses and anxieties. It would therefore be reasonable to look at the benefits of religious beliefs to a society or community and compare them with the benefits of coping strategies in an individual person, as that person grows and matures.

Here arises an interesting comparison. In any individual, coping strategies that help the person at an early stage of development may later be abandoned or totally reconstructed. They change as the individual grows and matures.

In the history of each of us as individuals, the things that helped us cope when we were children (dolls, security blankets, nightlights and so on) usually evolve into more and more abstract strategies in our minds. Eventually, simply the memory or image of a childhood object may give us comfort instead of the object itself. Hence, as we grow older we need fewer of the concrete objects of our childhood, and more and more sophisticated concepts to help us cope. A physical object that we use in a coping strategy and later abandon is called in psychiatric terms a "transitional object."

A comparable process has been going on, and is still going on, with religious beliefs on the much larger scale of humankind as a species. If the history of humankind can be compared in some ways to the growth of an individual human (in other words, if one could compare the process of civilization to the process of the maturation of an individual), the concept of god might be comparable to the function of a transitional object. It works in the same way as a childhood teddy bear or a security blanket: it is something that is perpetually by your side early in life and gives you comfort during periods of stress and change. Then it becomes subjected to change itself, as the individual learns new coping strategies and becomes more independent of the transitional object.

The evolving role of religion in society (from a monolithic state of everyone-believing-the-same-thing-ism to the current range of widely varied and highly personal belief systems) may be analogous to that changing function of the transitional object. The evolution of the figure of god from a heavenly, omnipotent, man-shaped giant-in-the-sky to a more abstract and personal motive force or essence may perhaps be compared to the natural evolution of a coping strategy and to the way that we, as individuals, use a transitional object for a time.

SUMMARY: BELIEF AS A UNIQUELY HUMAN ACTIVITY

In this chapter we have been looking at some of the benefits that a set of beliefs provides to the believer. Most of the points that I have raised are simply intuitive—you know that belief does this for the believer simply by thinking about it. The traits that I have discussed in this chapter are of course not the only ones (we shall discuss a few of the others in Chapter 6). But there are deep feelings and sensations that come from strong belief that are much more difficult to tabulate and categorize.

For example, a firm religious belief may give the believer not only a sense of divine destiny and justice but also a deep sense of personal calm and tranquility. The great majority of believers find the act of reflecting on the object of their belief—be it god or some other entity, external or internal—genuinely and deeply pleasurable; in many cases, the sense of pleasure and fulfillment found is deeper here than with any other activity. In fact, in several religions that is the entire point of communication with god: the act of prayer is viewed entirely as a method of changing the praying person's attitude and feelings. If the person achieves that sense of deep calm and tranquility, then the prayer—and hence the religion—is working. So the tendency to hold a firm belief in something is not only deeply ingrained, it is also deeply rewarding and satisfying.

We can draw some other conclusions from this material, too. First (as Campbell and Frazer both illustrated so brilliantly), there are obvious parallels and similarities among the myths and legends that express the beliefs of different communities and cultures. Many themes are common in the religious stories of many different countries, and presumably evolved separately and independently.

Even more significantly, concepts and images of god have undergone change and evolution over time. This change, as we have seen, can be compared to the change in coping strategies that occur in a person during growth and maturation, and to that extent, the function of religions may be seen as analogous to that of transitional objects in an individual's growth and maturation.

Finally, we can see that there are ways that beliefs in various objects or people differ one from another. This activity that we call "believing" is not a simple on/off function. There are various degrees of it: there are different intensities, different modes, methods and ways of believing.

One theme underlies many of these beneficial effects that accrue to the believer from the act of believing. Perhaps the most important of these combines justice with victory over death, over adversity and over persecution: it is the deep longing that humans share to be rescued. It is the strong hope that we all have for salvation and a saviour. We all (or almost all) want to be rescued, and so we personify that hope, in a fable or a fairy tale, a myth or legend. Some commentators believe that this is where religious beliefs originate. In fact, the continuity between those two processes—the expression of hope in myth or fable on the one hand, and religious belief on the other—is set out clearly by Joseph Campbell in *The Hero with a Thousand Faces* when he writes:

> It is obvious that the infantile fantasies, which we all cherish still in the unconscious, play continually into myth, fairy tale and the teachings of the church, as symbols of indestructible being. This is helpful, for the mind feels at home with the images and seems to be remembering something already known. But the circumstance is obstructive too, for the feelings come to rest in the symbols and resist passionately every effort to go beyond.

Campbell expresses a clear and important thought here, emphasizing the values of myth as well as the potential dangers. First, he observes that fairy tales and myths are part of a continuum that embraces religion, that they "play continually into" the teachings of the church. Second, he sees the value and the comfort of those images—which we seem to recognize and have already known—up to a certain point. Beyond that point they become an obstacle to our understanding and coping if the concept becomes too rigidly bound up in the symbol.

Now we can ask why.

Why is all of this so central to the way our species thinks and talks about the world? The answer is contained in the next chapter, in which I am going to set out some important evidence about the way the brain works and how it facilitates the feelings of external intelligence, deities and spiritual beings.

CHAPTER FOUR

The Mind of God and the God of Mind

So far, we've been talking about the social functions and the social effects of belief: how beliefs have been a part of what binds communities of humans together. (In this sense, beliefs act as cohesive forces, and thus, perhaps, offer a survival advantage in evolutionary terms.)

That discussion has been, as it were, at the social level of humankind's organization—we have been viewing belief at the anthropological, archaeological and historical levels. But there are other levels at which these issues can be discussed.

First, there is some important and relatively new evidence from neurological studies suggesting that what is sometimes experienced as the voice of god (or gods) is associated with activity in a particular area of the brain. Second, one can look at belief in an external deity in psychological terms by examining the experiences of a child as he or she grows up and looking at the ways that parental influences shape the child's system of beliefs. These two themes will be the focus of this chapter.

"HARD-WIRED": THE NEUROLOGY OF THEOLOGY

TEMPLES AND TEMPORALS

It has been known for a very long time that the temporal lobes of the brain are really quite different from its other areas: what goes on inside them is complex, subtle and rather peculiar.

The human brain consists, basically, of two main units: a deep central part (including the brainstem, where most of our life-sustaining functions are monitored and regulated) and the familiar cauliflower bit, which consists of the two cerebral hemispheres sitting on top

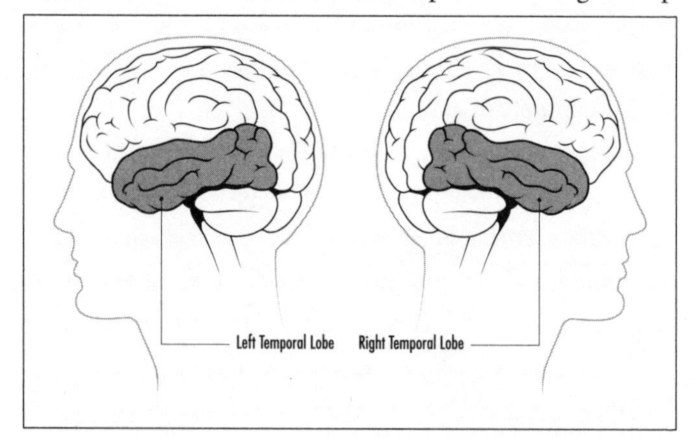

of and surrounding the deep central part. It is the two cerebral hemispheres that make the shape that you always see in cartoons and diagrams.

Each cerebral hemisphere is divided into several areas or lobes. The temporal lobes—one on each side, left and right—are the bits of your cerebral hemispheres that are inside your temples (hence their name). If you make a fist and put it just in front of your ear and level with the top of it, the bit of your brain under the area covered by your fist (approximately) is your temporal lobe.

The left temporal lobe functions as a major component of your language skills and (depending on the part of it we are talking about) some aspects of your motor skills. Damage in this area (for example from a stroke or a head injury) usually produces major difficulties with speech (as with aphasia or dysphasia) or certain types of difficulties in moving or doing things (sometimes called a dyspraxia).

Until a few decades ago, it was not entirely clear what the temporal lobe on the right side of your brain (whether you are right-handed or left-handed) actually did. But it was evidently quite complex and subtle, something to do with the person's interpretation of stimuli (hearing, taste and so on), as well as something to do with the person's perception of reality and of himself or herself.

It has also been known for a long time that the deeper

areas of the temporal lobes are part of a group of very important structures that together make up the limbic system. For that reason, some authorities call the deeper front-end part of the temporal lobes the limbic lobes. The limbic system includes two structures (one in each temporal lobe), each of which is a very important collection of brain cells located deep inside the temporal lobe and somewhat towards the front end of it. This structure is called the amygdaloid nucleus (which simply means that it is shaped like an almond), and the two of them are usually referred to jointly as the amygdala.

These components—the amygdala, the deeper parts of the temporal lobes plus some other structures—make up the limbic system. You can think of the limbic system as a very complex network of information-processing stations that handles and processes a great deal of the information that comes into and out of the temporal lobes.

What the temporal lobes do is a very complicated subject. The evidence that has accumulated to explain their function—in health and disease—comes from many different sources, and all of it converges to create a truly coherent and extraordinary picture. The first part of this evidence comes from the experiences of people who have epilepsy (seizures) originating in the temporal lobe.

EPILEPSY (SEIZURES) OF THE TEMPORAL LOBE

For many decades it was known that problems in the right temporal lobe produce peculiar disturbances of perception and experiences. And years ago it was realized that many of the people who suffer from an unusual type of seizure or epileptic fit—different in many important ways from the common type of seizure—are in fact suffering from the effects of damage or disease in the temporal lobes.

Let me explain that in greater detail. The usual kind of seizures in adults is the type that originates in or near the areas of the brain that control movements of the limbs, trunk and head. These areas—the motor areas—are situated in the top part of the parietal lobes (roughly speaking, the highest part of your brain when you are upright).

These seizures, starting in the motor areas, produce spasms (convulsions) of the limbs and usually go on to produce spasms that involve the whole body, followed by a short period of unconsciousness. The seizures are not usually harmful or serious in themselves (unless the person is engaged in activity or in a place where harm can result from losing consciousness), although they are alarming to the person who suffers them and to people nearby.

Seizures like these have been known and recognized

for hundreds of years (they are described in ancient Greek writings and in the New Testament). It has also been known for centuries that injuries to the motor areas in the brain and tumours in those areas are quite likely to cause this type of seizure. In the 1940s, when the electroencephalogram (EEG) was invented and it became possible to record the electrical activity in different parts of the brain, it became obvious that particular kinds of spasmodic electrical activity in the motor areas were the cause of these convulsions. In other words, electrical disturbances in these parts of the brain were the cause of the epileptic seizures.

But certain people have different seizures entirely. In this less common type, the first symptoms (usually called the "aura" of a seizure) include some very particular sensations and experiences. These may include any (or several) of the following: auditory hallucinations (hearing voices), déjà vu (the feeling of having seen something before), visual hallucinations, experiencing funny smells, a feeling of particular peace, a sensation of deep understanding or of profound and significant knowledge and a feeling of being outside one's own body. These episodes are often followed by a period of dream-like absence or unconsciousness similar to the experience that follows the usual type of seizure.

This pattern—of a particular aura usually including

a disturbance of perception, experience or a hallucination—is well recognized in neurology. The person who really initiated our modern attitude to this sort of seizure was a pioneer in neurology called Dr. Hughlings Jackson. Jackson made accurate and careful observations of many thousands of his patients with all types of seizures, and he correlated the seizures with what was found later on at autopsy after the patient had died. As a result of his groundbreaking work, the more common rhythmic seizures involving the limbs are called Jacksonian seizures. However, Jackson also showed that seizures of the less common type can be linked to damage or abnormalities in the temporal lobes. Furthermore, when the aura is more complex, involving perceptions, experiences, feelings and so on, usually the damaged or abnormal area is in the right temporal lobe. (When the left temporal lobe is involved, the seizures are more often accompanied by motor abnormalities and also by disturbances of memory.)

So Jackson's data established a clear and firm connection between abnormality or damage in the right temporal lobe and these peculiar experiences and changes in perception preceding a seizure. This connection became even clearer and more firmly established when the EEG was invented. As EEG studies began, it became immediately obvious that patients with these seizures had EEG patterns showing electrical abnormalities in the temporal lobe areas. Furthermore, when these people were given particular medications (different from the usual anticonvulsants) with specific power to control the abnormal seizure activity of the temporal lobe, the symptoms diminished or disappeared in most cases.

Thus, the three features of the temporal lobe were proven to be linked: (a) the symptoms of particular seizures causing episodic abnormalities of perception, (b) abnormal electrical activity in the temporal areas on the EEG and (c) improvement or disappearance of the symptoms and of the EEG abnormalities in many cases when appropriate medication was given.

Some neurologists, looking back at history, believe that temporal lobe epilepsy was the medical condition that caused Joan of Arc to have her visions of the Archangel Michael and to hear the voices—including the voice of God—that told her what to do. Similar symptoms were recorded centuries later by the Russian author Fyodor Dostoevsky, who also had temporal lobe epilepsy (as we would now call his seizures); he too described feelings of great peace and the sensation of an extracorporeal essence and of an all-embracing knowledge and understanding:

> All of the forces of life gathered convulsively all at once to the highest attainable consciousness.

> The sensation of life, of being, multiplied tenfold at that moment: all passion, all doubts, all unrests were resolved as in a higher peace: then a peace full of dear, harmonious joy and hope. And then a scene suddenly as if something were opening up in the soul; an indescribable, an unknown light radiated, by which the ultimate essence of things was made visible and recognizable. All this lasted at most a second.[1]

(Dostoevsky also wrote many extraordinary and brilliant descriptions of those experiences in his fiction, for example in his famous novel *The Idiot*.)

WHAT HAPPENS WHEN THE TEMPORAL LOBE IS STIMULATED

So, the first line of evidence came from what happened when there was a disorder of the temporal lobe. The second line of evidence came from experiences reported by patients when the temporal lobe was electrically stimulated during brain surgery.

Direct stimulation

This might sound barbaric—but it isn't! When a patient needs brain surgery (for example, to remove

1. See E. Murray and T.J. Murray, "The Epilepsy of Dostoevsky," *The Nova Scotia Medical Bulletin* (1980): 90–94.

a tumour) it is extremely important that the surgeon not damage healthy areas of the brain. The techniques required to avoid such damage were the main work of the Montreal neurosurgeon Dr. Wilder Penfield.

The brain itself does not feel pain, so Penfield performed neurosurgery under local anaesthesia with the patient awake (and feeling fine). Once the surface of the brain was exposed, Penfield applied low-voltage electric stimuli to various parts of the brain and asked the patient what he or she felt, or observed if there was movement of any limb. In this way—and it was groundbreaking work of immense importance—Penfield mapped out the functions of the various areas of the brain.

When he stimulated the motor areas, patients experienced involuntary movements or twitches of the arm or leg or lips or some other part of the body. But when he stimulated the temporal lobe on the right side, there was no movement of any part of the body. Instead, the patients reported a wide variety of significant experiences, perceptions and/or feelings. The phenomena reported were basically the same as the auras accompanying temporal lobe seizures—feelings of great peace, of deep understanding, of consciousness of another being, of sensations of taste, smell, sight or sound, and so on.

So here was further evidence that the right temporal lobe was involved in the complex process of perception and of consciousness (of self and of "non-self"). Further studies confirming Penfield's observations were made by members of the Montreal group and other neuroscientists.

At this point, then, the conclusion was inescapable: the right temporal lobe is a crucial component in our process of perception—in all modalities—and in the process by which we are conscious of ourselves and of things around us.

The next stage took this study beyond the experience of patients with epilepsy and into the general population.

Stimulation by magnetic signals

The neuroscientist who has done most of the recent major studies on the right temporal lobe is Dr. Michael Persinger of Laurentian University in Sudbury, Ontario. Persinger has specialized in research on the temporal lobe for nearly twenty years, and his results add up to a single consistent picture of what the temporal lobes do and how they affect our sense of ourselves and of external beings.[2]

Perhaps the best place to start is by talking about his experiments in applying electromagnetic signals to the brain—from the outside, by setting up magnetic fields around the head.

2. M.A. Persinger, "Religious and Mystical Experiences as Artifacts of Temporal Lobe Function: A General Hypothesis," *Perceptual and Motor Skills* (1983): 1,255–62.

Persinger has focused on research into the electromagnetic "language" of the brain, and how it is employed in memory, in interpreting the outside world and in consciousness. What makes his work so important is that he and his group have started the process of imitating the electromagnetic signals that the brain uses, and then "playing back" those imitations to human brains to see what happens.

The crucial part of Persinger's experiment is the nature of the electromagnetic field that he uses. Over a long series of experiments, he has designed various electromagnetic signals—based, for example, on the waveforms created by the right temporal lobe in patients with temporal lobe epilepsy. These signals are very short, are repeated after a pause of a certain length, have certain "shapes" and so on.

Perhaps it can be compared to trying to work out what people do when they read a book. Say you were an alien from another planet, and you couldn't speak the same language as your subjects and couldn't communicate with them directly. If you wanted to investigate the act of reading among humans you might start with the observation that people read by looking at black print on a white page (that might change in the future, but it's the most common format for reading at the moment). To find out more about reading, you would need to see what happens when you put words on a printed page in front of a person. You would need "proper" words—and therein lies the crucial part of your investigation. You wouldn't get very far if you introduced a test object comprising a white piece of paper with a big black blob in the middle of it. This would not make a very interesting read for the reader—who would ignore it—and your test would be an absolute dud.

The same sort of strictures apply to investigating the brain's signalling system—in order to find out how it works, you need to use the electromagnetic equivalent of "words" (or at least "letters"), not merely big black blobs on white paper. If you give a brain a single flat magnetic signal, it will ignore it—and rightly so!

Persinger and his group set about creating electromagnetic fields (generated by computers) with very specific shapes and time intervals, and then fed these pulsed signals to solenoids (cylindrical coils of wire acting as magnets when carrying electric current), thus creating electromagnetic fields. The solenoids were then mounted in pairs, one placed opposite the other in a helmet that the volunteer wore.

When the volunteers were exposed to these specific low-intensity electromagnetic fields concentrated over the right temporal lobe, the results were exactly what

Persinger had been hoping for. The volunteers experienced the same sorts of effects noted by patients with temporal lobe epilepsy and by patients undergoing Penfield's neurosurgical studies. They saw and experienced and felt particular sensations.[3]

Sometimes the sensations were visual or auditory; sometimes they were complex experiences; sometimes they were based on actual memories; sometimes they were fundamental and deep-rooted feelings. Many of them, however, had to do with a feeling of peace, of serenity, of being at one with nature and often of being in the presence of another consciousness (another being). Some people felt they were near the presence of aliens. Others experienced deeply spiritual or religious feelings. Some reported that they felt they were in the presence of god, and some heard his voice.

The Persinger continuum of temporal lobe sensitivity

This was fascinating, but there was more to come. Persinger's group then used the electromagnetic stimulation system to probe further into how the right temporal lobe affects human experience—and found something of major importance.

3. L.A. Ruttan, M.A. Persinger and S. Koren, "Enhancement of Temporal Lobe-Related Experiences During Brief Exposures to Milligauss Intensity Extremely Low Frequency Magnetic Fields," *J Bioelectricity* 9 (1990): 33–54.

They found that there is a continuum of temporal lobe sensitivity, from people with clearly diagnosed medical conditions to the general population. At the top end of the sensitivity scale, people with temporal lobe epilepsy have (as you would expect) extremely sensitive temporal lobes—so sensitive that they fire off by themselves without any stimulus (which is the cause of the epileptic seizure).[4] People with slightly less sensitive lobes are the kind of people who have "absences" or episodes, sometimes switching off from the real world for a moment or two.

Then there are people who are able to fully "get into" an imaginary world readily. Persinger tested a group of poets and found that they had temporal lobes that were much more sensitive than the average. The same was true of drama students. This would make sense, since acting requires the ability to imagine what it would be like to be someone else, and to inhabit an imaginary world for a time.

4. We know a little about this process, too. It is called recruitment—and the more nerves that are recruited into an electrical discharge, the higher the chance of the discharge resulting in a seizure. Studies by many neuroscientists (in line with Persinger's studies) show that if a large percentage of nerve cells become recruited, comparable to a big avalanche—in fact, over 20 per cent of those nerve cells in the area—a seizure will occur. If more than 7 per cent or so are recruited, the result is a mini-seizure, which is not recognizable as a true (or major) seizure by the patient or the doctor. In the temporal lobe area these are called TLEPS (temporal lobe epileptiform partial seizures)—they are recognizable on the EEG and the patient experiences certain episodes at the time. Complex Partial Epileptic-Like experiences (CPELs) are a sign of an irritable or sensitive temporal lobe.

When Persinger's group performed these tests on various groups of people and correlated the results with their subjects' religious experiences, they found that there was a fairly close relationship: the more sensitive your temporal lobe is, the more likely it is that you will have regular (and deep) religious experiences.

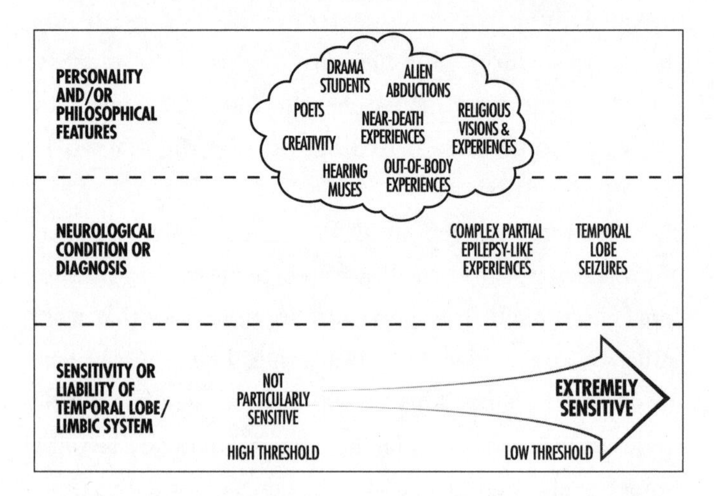

Every single one of us has a threshold level of sensitivity inbuilt into our right temporal lobe. If you are a person who happens to have an extremely low level for that threshold (meaning that your temporal lobe is extremely sensitive), it will fire off by itself and you will suffer from temporal lobe epilepsy (you might call this a spontaneously discharging temporal lobe). If it happens that your threshold is a bit higher but still much lower than the average, then you will have odd episodes and experiences but not recognizable epileptic seizures. If your temporal lobes are less sensitive than that but still more sensitive than the average, you will be a relatively creative person—a poet or an actor, for example.[5]

Fizzes and quizzes

So, the right temporal lobe has its own "setting" of sensitivity in each of us, and this correlates with certain aspects of our experience and of our perceptions. Persinger and his co-worker Katherine Makarec then went on to see if they could identify any *specific* patterns of experience or behaviour that matched their observations. In other words, if a person has a particularly sensitive right temporal lobe, what are they likely to think, and what are they likely to feel?

They used a standardized questionnaire (it's called the Minnesota Multiphasic Personality Inventory) and then tested a large series of questions of their own to see if they could produce a reliable guide to the sensitivity of the right temporal lobe in the form of patterns of answering questions. The result was a tool that they called the Personal Philosophy Inventory (PPI), and it turned out to be

5. M.A. Persinger and K. Makarec, "Complex Partial Epileptic Signs As a Continuum from Normals to Epileptics: Normative Data and Clinical Populations," *J Clin. Psychology* 49 (1993): 33–45.

a very reliable and useful indicator of many features of a person's thought and behaviour, including indications of the sensitivity of the right temporal lobe. For example, some people have a particular type of episode that is similar to a brief (and less dramatic) mild version of a temporal lobe seizure. These episodes are called Complex Partial Epileptic-Like experiences (CPELs), and, sure enough, Persinger found that people who have CPELs could be identified by certain items on his PPI.[6]

So now, thanks to a series of experimental observations, we have an unquestionable chain of evidence that links the temporal lobe with a series of thoughts and attitudes specifically concerning spirituality, religiousness, perceptions of reality, readiness to feel the presence of another being and so on.

That chain of evidence—as I've explained—goes back to the first descriptions of temporal lobe seizures (like the ones later described by Dostoevsky), to the observations of Hughlings Jackson, to the experiments of Wilder Penfield and then to the electromagnetic field experiments of Persinger and his group and to the series of thoughts and attitudes tested on the questionnaires.

6. K. Malarec and M.A. Persinger, "Electroencephalographic Validation of a Temporal Lobe Signs Inventory in a Normal Population," *J Res. Personality* 24 (1990): 323–37.

Corroborating evidence

Further evidence supporting all these conclusions came from other methods of studying the brain. There are some ways of scanning that can show which areas of the brain are actually working. One of these methods is called a SPECT scan, in which an isotope is injected into the bloodstream and is tracked by a special system of scanning. These SPECT scans show which areas of the brain are working (e.g., using up glucose or oxygen) at that moment. Sure enough, when the person is having a religious or spiritual experience (or any of the other experiences listed above), it is the right temporal lobe that is seen on the SPECT scan to be in action.

The same is true of another method of brain imaging, the magnetic resonance imaging (MRI) scan. There is a special way of doing MRI scans so that the function of the different parts of the brain can be seen. This is called F-MRI scanning—and it shows the same results as the SPECT. When the person experiences the phenomena that have been listed above, the right temporal lobe shows activity, providing further corroboration of the Persinger hypothesis.

FEATURES ASSOCIATED WITH THE RIGHT TEMPORAL LOBE

If you take all the results of Persinger's studies together, they add up to a fascinating picture of what the right temporal lobe does. In summary form, the features of thinking and feeling that are associated with the right temporal lobe are:

- *auditory experiences:* hearing sounds or voices (auditory hallucinations), often speaking directly to you; sometimes these are voices of people from one's past
- *visual experiences:* seeing lights, patterns of light and dark, sometimes including the commonly cited white light at the end of the tunnel, sometimes entire images from one's past, including images of deceased relatives and friends
- *vestibular experiences*: the sense of whirling through space, going into a tunnel and other changes in orientation and position
- *taste and smell experiences*: sometimes smells that are familiar from the past, sometimes new ones
- *memory changes:* déjà vu (the sense of having seen something before, when one hasn't), jamais vu (the sense of never having seen something before, when one has)
- *extracorporeal experiences*: the sense of being outside one's own body
- *morning "highs":* people who get a "high" in the

morning have higher scores than average in temporal lobe signs

- *drama, poetry and other creative acts:* activities that require the person to "get into" another world or another mode are associated with high temporal lobe scores
- *sense of presence:* the feeling that one is in the presence of another intelligence, sometimes religious (god), sometimes alien
- *other religious and spiritual experiences:* many different kinds of deep and spiritual experiences, including a sense of peace, being at one with nature, understanding in some intangible way the working of the cosmos
- *signs of special significance:* the feeling that various things that happen in the world are specific signals directed at the person
- *pseudocyesis (false pregnancy):* women who have experiences of cessation of menstrual periods, enlarging abdomen and breast changes (when they are not in fact pregnant) have high scores on temporal lobe signs
- *near-death experiences:* the white light and the sense of peace often associated with near-death experiences (e.g., drowning or hypothermia)

- *"I would kill in God's name"*: this is a very important feature of temporal lobe activity and will be discussed in detail in Chapter 6.

THE BICAMERAL MIND

Before we leave this subject, I would like to highlight an important way that these results link up with some earlier theories about the way the human mind works.

In 1962, a scientist, historian and thinker named Julian Jaynes popularized the idea that our minds all work in a "right-brain/left-brain" manner. Of course the fact that the human brain consists of two halves was well known, but Jaynes examined the differing and complementary activities of the two halves and backed up his view with neurological, as well as archeological and historical, data. In *The Origins of Consciousness in the Breakdown of the Bicameral Mind*, Jaynes comes to some startling conclusions.

He suggests that consciousness—awareness of one's self as a person and personality—did not evolve steadily or even early in humankind's history. Jaynes suggests that what we nowadays regard as "our own thoughts" were originally perceived by the thinker as voices coming from the spirits of dead ancestors. Jaynes proposed that thoughts originating in the right side of the brain crossed over into the left, where they were not recognized as the person's own but seemed to arrive from outside.

The neurological facts and theories underpinning the idea of transfer from one side to the other are widely accepted now. Perhaps some of Jaynes's historical data are more controversial—he believes that the use of different words for "soul" or "spirit" or "mind" showed that consciousness "arrived" quite suddenly in early Greek times—but the overall concept of the two-chambered (bicameral) mind sending information from one side to the other is of great importance.

The convergence of Jaynes's hypothesis (and supporting data) with the neuroscience of Penfield and Persinger is significant, and it provides a considerable measure of validation for both methods of looking at brain function. What Jaynes deduced from our history and neuroanatomy lends support to the observations of modern neuroscience.

WHAT DOES ALL THIS MEAN?

Taken together, the experiments of Penfield and Persinger and many others, along with the theories of Jaynes, are of exceptional consequence, because they show that the temporal lobe is a crucial factor in many complex experiences and feelings. In particular, the experience of being close to, or in the company of, an external benign intelligence—whether it is a god or an alien—is one of these experiences that can be produced by electrical stimulation of the brain itself, or by special magnetic fields applied over the skull.

Now, this does *not*, of course, prove that belief in the presence of god is merely or entirely a property of a piece of brain tissue. In themselves, these results do not prove that god does not exist and is simply a product of the brain. After all, almost any subjective sensation can be produced by stimulation of the correct part of the brain, and this does not negate the real experience when it happens. For example, you might stimulate my occipital lobes and I would see bright lights—but that does not mean that when, in everyday life, I see a bright light there is no light actually there. When a light is flashed into my eyes, signals reach my occipital lobes and I interpret those signals as evidence that a light has flashed on somewhere in the outside world in front of my eyes. The fact that the same interpretation can *also* be produced by direct stimulation of those lobes does not disprove the existence of flashing lights. The same is true of the right temporal lobe and the experience of god. It is just telling us something about the way our brains are designed—and that is in itself neither bad nor good in any sense.

Let me use another example to illustrate what I'm saying—and to support the idea that knowing more about our brain's design neither belittles us nor aggrandizes us.

This is an illusion that probably most of you already know. You might even have used it as a party trick. Ask a friend to cross his middle finger over his index finger (as in the time-honoured gesture of hoping for something). Get him to close his eyes, and then slide a pencil along the V-shaped crook of his crossed fingers back and forth a few times. Ask him what he feels: is there one pencil or two? If he has his eyes closed, it will feel as if there are two pencils.

This is a simple illusion, and it is caused by the fact that the brain interprets information from the outside

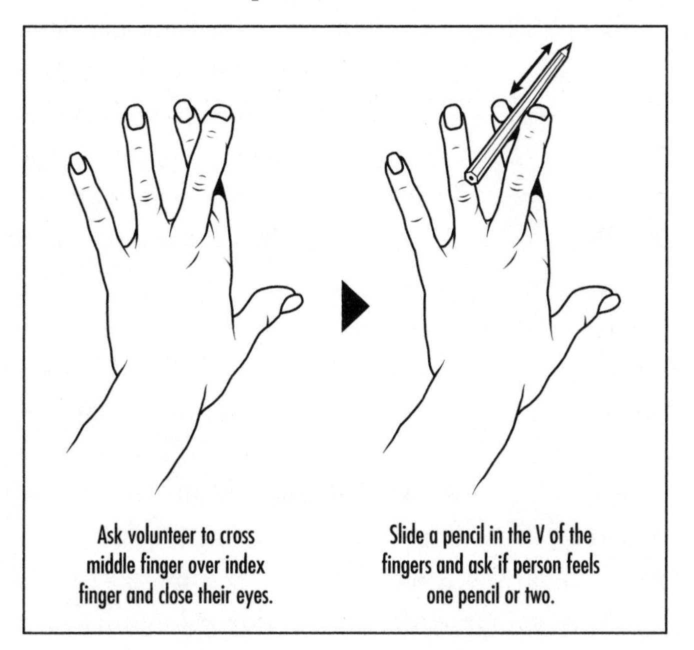

surface of two fingers in a certain way. Normally (when your fingers are not crossed) when the brain receives "something is touching skin" signals from the thumb side of the index finger and the ring-finger side of the middle finger, it means that there are two "somethings," each making contact with a finger at the same moment. When a person crosses his or her fingers, the brain can't override that impression with the new piece of information that the fingers are crossed. Hence, it interprets the signals as a two-pencil situation. It can't do anything else—it's the way the brain is hard-wired.

This illusion plays on a simple fact of human physiology. Its implications are not derogatory, and it doesn't challenge our concept of free will or suggest that our brains are "faulty" or "malfunctioning." It's just a quirk or idiosyncrasy of the way our neural system is set up. Equally, the universality of the perception does not create a new reality. The fact that every single human being will feel as if there are two pencils there does not mean that there are actually two pencils there. It simply shows that being human means that when your fingers are crossed you will perceive one pencil as two. The illusion is telling us something about particular patterns of perception built into our brains; it's telling us something about the way human beings interpret the world.

The same is true with all the temporal lobe data we

have been discussing in this chapter. These observations do not demean or insult human minds; they don't prove that we are faulty machines or that we are constructed on a bedrock of neurological errors and glitches. These data—like the pencil trick—tell us something about the way our brains are hard-wired to interpret the world. The observations tells us something about the patterns that are built into our limbic systems, in the same way the pencil trick tells us something about our tactile sensory inputs. It is important for us all to acknowledge these facts about ourselves and our brains—we are built to think "two pencils" when our fingers are crossed, and that doesn't matter very much. We are also built to readily perceive the presence of an external intelligence and other extracorporeal phenomena, and in the vast majority of situations that doesn't matter much either, but in some circumstances it can matter a great deal (as we will discuss in Chapter 6). The important point is to acknowledge the observations and accept what they are telling us about our brain's modus operandi. We can't change it, but the more we learn about it the better it will be for all of us.

NOT "JUST" ELECTRICITY AND CHEMICALS

One final point before we leave this topic: this general hypothesis about the right temporal lobe does not rob human imagination of spirituality or meaning. An emotion or experience might be created by or mediated by the right temporal lobe, but that does not mean that spirituality or experiences of nature (or anything else) are "just" the temporal lobe or "nothing but a low voltage passing through a slab of brain."

The Victorian poet Samuel Taylor Coleridge was an opium addict. After a particularly constructive dose of opium one day, he had a vision of magic palaces and mysterious potentates and sat down and started writing the beginning of a wonderful poem, "Kubla Khan." (As a matter of interest, he was interrupted by a visitor from a town called Porlock who bored him for a long time. When he returned to his poem the vision had gone completely, and "Kubla Khan" remains a fragment—a thought that has always worried me whenever I ring the doorbell of a writer or a poet.) The poem is a great poem, no matter whether its creation was precipitated or engendered by opium or not. "Kubla Khan" is not "merely opium." If you were told that Mozart or T. S Eliot or James Joyce had some specific psychiatric complaint, that wouldn't diminish his work in the least. It would be interesting, and it might add to your thoughts about his life, but it wouldn't make you dismiss his works.

The same is true of everything we have been discussing in this chapter so far. If the right temporal lobe is the main pathway for spiritual experience, this does not remove the significance, the beauty, the meaning or the value of spiritual experience (or of any of the artworks inspired by it). It is an explanation of the mechanism, and is not a dismissive summary of the result.

OUR FATHER: PARENTAL INFLUENCES

Thus far, then, we have seen that the design of the brain—specifically of the right temporal lobe—makes it very easy for us to have religious experiences. But even if that tendency is inbuilt into our brains, why is it activated so often in so many people? Even if we all have inherent leanings to undergo spiritual experiences, why is it that so often those experiences end up with a particular view of an extracorporeal divine figure of a god that controls us and our destiny? Let me attempt an explanation.

Imagine, just for the moment, that what Persinger and his antecedents and colleagues are saying is true. Imagine that humans are born with an inbuilt tendency or propensity to think that there is an extracorporeal intelligence, a Something that is Out There making things happen. Even if that tendency is built into the basic structure of the human mind, how did it become such an important component of the way humans perceive the world? What powers exercise and strengthen that tendency, and nurture and encourage its development?

The answer has been stated many times in psychiatry (notably since the pioneering work of Freud, who based most of his methodology on it). We are all moulded—from the time of our earliest glimmerings of consciousness—by our parents or parent substitutes. They draw our map of the world, whether they mean to or not—and that map or system gives us a model on which we later base our concepts of god.

Let me expand on that.

When you are a baby, your biggest problem is that you don't have much control over the world or over what happens to you. If you feel hungry, you can't just make yourself a sandwich or grab a cookie; the only thing you can do is to cry (after all, you haven't yet learned to ask for anything in words or signs). But when you cry, an amazing thing happens. A huge human comes towards you, often smiling, and depending on its gender and methodology, it might give you a breast or a bottle. Either way, your inner needs have been met. Your unspoken wishes have been granted. Miracle!

As you get older, you learn that there are certain things you do that will earn you the opposite of rewards.

Sometimes the consequence will be merely the absence of a smile; on other occasions it will involve harsh, loud sounds being aimed at you; in some instances (depending on your culture and community) you might even be slapped.

From your earliest helpless moments, then, you become aware of a vast, powerful figure who metes out reward and punishment in response to (so it appears to you) your merest wishes or thoughts. When you do things that are wrong you receive punishment (the "stick"), and you are encouraged to do things that are accepted as good for which you are rewarded (the "carrot").

Then, as you grow up and acquire language and start asking questions about the world, you are told about something your parents heard from their parents—a god that reads your innermost thoughts and wishes and hands out reward and punishment. It makes perfect sense to you, and no wonder. Your earliest experiences from your parents have given you an intuitive model of being looked after by a caring, benign, powerful figure. Perhaps, therefore, it is no coincidence that god is often spoken of as a parental figure.

The importance of this connection between parental influence and preparedness for later belief systems cannot be overstated. The one thing we *all* share is the fact that we started out as helpless babies. We owe the fact that we are alive today to somebody's actions in fending for us when we had no power to fend for ourselves. The image of an eternal parent who has powers that we cannot comprehend—but who will look after us in our own best interests and administer appropriate carrots and sticks—is imprinted on us from birth. We can hardly think of any other model for our concept of a deity. We learned it at our parent's knee. Our parents are our first gods.

SUMMARY: GOD AS A STATE OF MIND

The experiments of Drs. Jackson, Penfield and Persinger and others that I have been discussing lead us to an important—and inescapable—conclusion: the structure of the human brain is such that experiences of god and heaven are hard-wired into it. Our brains lead us to readily undergo experiences that we have chosen to call god or spirituality or oneness-with-the-universe or similar words or names. If the limbic system is activated by means of the right temporal lobe, a person will have an experience of the spiritual or divine type. God is—literally—a state of mind.

Of course, as I stated above, this does *not* necessarily mean that god is *only* a state of mind. That is an entirely different subject, and beyond the mandate of this book. As I have said plainly several times, this book is not about the existence or the non-existence of god; it is about the causes and effects of our need to believe. I need to state again clearly that—even with the conclusions reached by Persinger's research—it is still *possible* that there is an external deity outside human life, and that contact with this external deity requires that the recipient's mind be in a certain state. It is possible also that the state necessary to make that contact is (fortunately for the believer) hard-wired into the design of the human brain. These things are possible—although, of course, in my personal view, they are most unlikely.

The really important point of these observations is that there is undeniable evidence that our brains are set up to "tell" us that there is an external deity. We are programmed to undergo experiences and feelings that we call religious or divine or god. We are built that way.

Once we realize that fact, we can still decide for ourselves whether there is (or is not) Something or Someone out there who communicates with us when we are in the appropriate mental state. However, we all—theists and non-theists—need to acknowledge the fact that the human brain is designed and patterned to suggest to us that there is an external god, whether there is one or not.

Perhaps (as was stated during the birth of modern nuclear physics), our dramatic progress in understanding the physical nature of the universe is somewhat like seeing into the mind of god. I cannot say whether that is true or not. I can, however, say unequivocally that the *experience* of god is built into the human mind.

The god of mind is undeniable; the mind of god is the subject of a continuing debate.

PART TWO

Behaving

CHAPTER FIVE

The Story So Far: From the Top Downwards

"RELIGION: COULD DO BETTER"

If you were an anthropologist visiting this planet from, say, Alpha Centauri, and if you had the opportunity to look over humankind's entire history and its current state, you might conclude that religion has not been an unalloyed benefit for the species.

Perhaps, if you were writing a report card on humankind, in the box marked "religious activities" you might give it a C– grade. Your comment might be something to the effect that religion was "not a *total* disaster (so far, anyway), but there have been major problems: there is clearly a great deal of room for improvement." Or something like that, anyway.

It might occur to you that given the frequently explosive history of this planet's religions, concepts of god have always had the *potential* for inciting violence and strife. (In the same way, you might reflect, that dynamite always has a potential for causing explosions even when there is no explosion in progress at that moment.)

In this chapter and the next, we are going to look at the report card for humankind's religious activities—the pluses and the minuses. We will start in this chapter by looking at the benefits—the "pro" points—that religious beliefs have brought to human behaviour. In the next chapter, we'll look at some of the problems—the "con" points.

GOOD COMMANDMENTS FOR FALLIBLE HUMANS

By and large, religious codes of behaviour brought varying (usually high) degrees of organization and conformity to early communities, which were somewhat chaotic at the time, and which comprised disparate individuals probably behaving in an arbitrary way for most of the time. Religion brought a measure of order. No religion failed to do that.

Every religion impressed upon its adherents the need to uphold certain fundamental principles. These were derived from the community's concept of the deity and always contained important strictures on the behaviour of the followers. In Jewish and in Christian religions, of course, the most important codes of behaviour are contained in the Bible and exemplified in the Ten Commandments. Like those of most religions, these statutes are thought to have originated with the deity and to have been transmitted via prophets (Moses and others), or, in other religions, the elders or the chosen holy persons. Such statutes and rules are therefore based on "revealed truths," or truths delivered from on high to the select, as opposed to "derived truths," truths arrived at from observations of the way humans actually behave.

In general, most of these revealed-truth rules were very good. They enshrined codes of socially desirable behaviour that achieved several benefits for the community. The codes introduced a measure of uniformity among the members, which acted as a cohesive force in the community and helped members align their expectations of each other. If you knew what action your religion called for in a given set of circumstances, then you knew (roughly) what to expect from those around you when those circumstances arose. Thus religious rules—like any rules accepted by a community—reduced the levels of surprise, perplexity and annoyance in social interactions. And since religious codes informed the members overtly of the types of behaviour regarded as socially desirable, they therefore added to the psychological rewards when people behaved in accordance with the statutes. Thus, in themselves, god-given statutes generally helped communities that shared the same vision of a deity to run more efficiently and smoothly.

The problems came, of course, when one community encountered another that worshipped a totally different deity and had a different set of rules of behaviour, and therefore had different expectations of people's behaviour. (We will discuss that further in Chapter 6.)

The central point here is that early in the development of human communities, god-given statutes were of great value in advancing conformity, uniformity of expectations and vision, and reducing arbitrary, ad hoc behaviour. They played an important part in melding a number of independent individuals into a group—in other words, in creating a true community.

It is no exaggeration to say that religious rules were a major force in the process that we call civilization.

COMMUNITY AND THE GENUINE SENSE OF BELONGING

Let us discuss that sense of community a little further. Like all cohesive forces that bind community members together, religion has produced enormous benefits for its adherents as a group. This is an aspect of religion that is extremely important and valuable: it must never be underrated or demeaned. Religion has always played a vital role in the development and evolution of a community (whether or not the divinity at the centre of that religion actually exists). Almost all religions have provided (at some stage in their evolution) a set of clear and coherent guidelines with which a group of people can work together, and there is considerable value in that. When people are engaged in a conjoint effort and are following clearly understood communal objectives, carrying out activities that are rooted in, and shaped by, the culture of that community, it produces considerable reward and goodwill. The people who are doing that activity always experience something (whether it is originally derived from the "instincts of the herd" or not) that makes them feel valued and valuable. They are contributing, and they are among "kindred spirits."

This effect on self-esteem is a feature of all truly communal activity, and at present most non-theists do not have a satisfactory substitute for the cohesive rewards of religious activity on a large scale. A few non-theist organizations do offer congregational activities that give a true sense of community, and it is extremely valuable. However, most individual non-theists don't have that sense of belonging to a community. Many of them speak of a genuine sense of isolation, a feeling of being the only person in the world who doesn't believe in an external deity.

RENDERING UNTO CAESAR: CHURCH AND STATE

There is another important point here, and that concerns the relationship between religion and community, between church and state. At a time when communities had reached a certain size and complexity, the "state" *was* the religious community, the nation *was* the church. Initially, this was not a problem. But things are different now, and I hope you'll forgive a bit of editorializing.

After many centuries, the continuation of church-state unity—aside from the great danger that religious doctrine that enters law can restrict freedom—started to make things very uncomfortable for any individuals who did not happen to share the generally accepted vision of a deity. If you weren't a member of the nation's church, you would be made to feel that you weren't a "proper" member of that state. The continuation of that feeling is, to this day, one of the problems that makes it difficult for individuals to "come out" about their own beliefs if they differ from the general ones. They feel that they are diminishing their personal membership in the state, and do feel that they are—as I've said—rather isolated. In my view this need not happen.

Things could be different—and the sense of community that so many people gain from conjoint religious observances can be gained when there is no religious event at the centre. Let me give you an example.

We all know and experience the particular sense of communal celebration when various festivals (e.g., Christmas, Thanksgiving) come around. Of course there are always a few extremely religious and traditional people who get upset that the original spirit of the festival (particularly Christmas, but other festivals are also subjected to this criticism) has been forgotten in the epidemic of commercial and prefabricated celebration. But—and I'm being distinctly heretical here—I'm not sure those people are right.

There is something to be said for a community celebrating in unison *any festival* of its own choosing. Any common celebration brings its own benefits and sense of belonging. For example, take Hallowe'en. Nowadays on the North American continent, Hallowe'en is a big deal. The kids look forward to it for months. Parents make or buy costumes. Most of the houses in the neighbourhood welcome the kids and give out candies. While the kids are reaping candy, their parents meet their neighbours (a few of whom they will only see at this time every year). People warm up and change their attitude to their community, and some of that feeling lasts for a long time.

Who cares that the festival originated with the ancient All Saints' Day? In fact, very few people even know that (nor did I, until I was educated on the subject). If a few people ever think about where Hallowe'en came from, mostly they tend to link it with the ancient German festival of Walpurgisnacht, the witches' Big Night Out (which is actually on April 30). Does it matter? Whether the origin of Hallowe'en is All Saints' Day, Witches Night or even Groundhog Day, does it alter the social function or the value to the community of the festival? Surely not. What is important is that genuine feeling or mood that runs through the community—it's palpable. It works on its own. The activity is valuable because it *works*.

In my view, pretty well any festival can have this effect, originally based on a religious theistic event or not. The sense of true community can, in my view, be separated from the religious devotion that originally brought the community together.

SUMMARY: "DO AS YOU ARE BADE"

To summarize, God-given statutes have a lot going for them: they are a very quick and effective way of regularizing a community's behaviour and increasing cohesion among its members. I would go so far as to say that humankind could not possibly have achieved such momentous advances in civilization in its comparatively short history were it not for the "shorthand" of religious codes of behaviour.

Most of the issues covered by religious codes of behaviour are extremely complex—"Thou shalt not kill" is a good example (and one that never seems to have worked particularly well). To educate each generation in the pros and cons of each of the statutes would have required an immense investment of time and effort (even if it were matched by knowledge and understanding). It was far more efficient and quick for a community to agree (for instance) that killing or stealing or adultery was wrong "because God says so." The divine and eternal punishment-reward system is clearly visible and intelligible to all—and that makes it a quick and efficient method of encouraging individuals to behave in a way that conforms to the needs and desires of the community.

So statutes that originate "from the top down" had a major and constructive role in hurrying humankind through issues that we nowadays would regard as highly complicated. Unfortunately, while they achieved that, they also precluded most of the elements of self-determination from the individual and initiated the endless debate on the existence of free will and God's intentions in creating it.

It would be fair to say that theist-derived codes of behaviour put humankind onto a fast track, but—as I shall examine in Chapters 7 and 8—we may now have reached a stage of maturity and development at which their disadvantages are close to outweighing their advantages.

CHAPTER SIX

The Dogma in the Manger: Some Problems Associated with Theism

> What we call rational grounds for our beliefs are often extremely irrational attempts to justify our instincts.
>
> —Thomas Henry Huxley (1825–1895)

RELIGION AND AGGRESSION: A CLOSE RELATIONSHIP OR COINCIDENCE?

Even from the perspective of a visiting anthropologist from Alpha Centauri, it would be quite clear that from its beginnings, religion has often been close to the source of considerable strife and divisiveness. In this chapter we will unpick some of the strands of those troubles and see how humankind's capacity to behave aggressively and violently is easily amplified and escalated by religious beliefs: how religion is an issue that readily helps the storm clouds break.

As I have implied in its title, this chapter is going to focus solely on the problems created by theist beliefs. I am not, of course, suggesting that *all* belief in a god must *inevitably* and *necessarily* lead to strife and aggression, but I am stressing the fact that since the beginnings of recorded history that is what has happened. Religion has frequently been used as a justification or a rationale for violence.

If our history had been different—if religious differences had generated no more violence and killing than, say, differing tastes in poetry or in cooking[1]—then I personally would not be concerned with it at all (and I would not bother writing a book on the subject). It is because religious beliefs have such a wartorn history that I am concerned with the connection between god and good in the first place.

We will start by examing some of our less cerebral and more reflex (or "animal") behaviours: things that we (and other species) do that originate from inbuilt urges and

1. Sometimes culinary tastes can actually lead to war. In *Gulliver's Travels*, Jonathan Swift describes the religious (his adjective!) war between the two kingdoms of Lilliput and Blefescu, which was prompted by the knotty decision as to which end of a boiled egg was the correct end to open first. Of course this is a ludicrous issue to go to war over, as I and the millions of other right-minded Little Enders would agree (and perhaps we would after all be prepared to kill any remaining Big Enders if they dared to oppose our views).

instincts rather than from conscious choices. Then we can look at some of the ways that we rationalize those instincts and ways that religion (among other systems of belief) has been used as a form of rationalization and justification for aggression. Finally we will turn to some of the experimental observations that show that the predisposition to perform aggressive acts in god's name is associated with certain traits located in the right temporal lobe of the brain.

So let us start with a few of the less cerebral instincts that underlie our inter-group conflict, mechanisms derived from the ways humans organize themselves into groups or tribes.

"WE ARE US—AND THEY ARE THEM": AGGRESSION AND INSTINCTS OF THE HERD

TURF AND WAR: TERRITORY AND TRIBE

The first step on the road to inter-group conflict is for a group to acquire its own identity, identifying itself as a unit (an "Us") as distinct from all other groups (which then become "Them"). When a collection of individuals do this, they are setting out on a road towards the recognition of themselves as a cohesive community and the recognition of the territory or land that they inhabit as "theirs." In other words, they start laying claim to their turf. (Of course, there is some evidence that it was the turf that gave the group its identity in the first place. It was when humans first started cultivating land that they became defensive and territorial in an internecine way.[2] From the point of view of this book, it is not important which came first, the group identity or turf ownership. It only matters that humans, their territories and their community identities all exist together now.)

A group that has acquired cohesion and now recognizes itself as a unit is—to use an impolite word—a herd. Since that process—cohesion and recognition—are crucial parts of any inter-group strife (including religious differences) that may follow, it is worth discussing group behaviour in some detail.

THEM-AND-US-ING: WHAT WE DO WHEN THERE ARE LOTS OF US

Group or crowd behaviour has always been a source of real problems for human societies. One of the earliest thoughtful works on this subject (and the reason I used the word "herd" above) was written in 1915 by a surgeon, Professor Wilfred Trotter. His book *Instincts of the Herd in Peace and War* was based on two articles that he

2. It is worth looking at Robert Ardrey's book *Territorial Imperative*. It is a highly quirky and idiosyncratic view, but worth a glance, and it deals with the way that much of the behaviour of many animal species is related to recognized territory.

had written in 1908 and 1909 (the dates are significant). He had been prompted to talk about the subject because of what he observed happening in the world as it primed itself for the First World War. His assessments and predictions proved to be accurate in the following years, unfortunately for everybody. Trotter's book is a masterpiece of clear thinking, and it was genuinely revolutionary for its time, changing the way that people thought about the influence of crowds and groups. In fact, it is one of those books that so patently sets the trend for the future that, in retrospect, it seems almost blindingly obvious (proving the old adage that "a successful revolution makes itself redundant").

Taking his cue from a few rather superficial observations of animal biology and looking for similarities in human behaviour (a controversial and chancy activity), Trotter felt that the three major instincts—self-preservation, food and sex—were insufficient to explain the totality of human behaviour. He thought a fourth major component of human behaviour was needed to explain our history. The fourth instinct, Trotter proposed, was gregariousness, the herd instinct. He was guessing—and he had not done much homework—but he was thinking logically, and as it turned out he was mostly right. I am not saying that Trotter was a particularly great or original ethologist, but he was probably the first to say publicly what everybody knew but had not previously admitted—namely, that humans behave differently when they are in a large group, and that some of these differences are not due to individual conscious decisions and choices but originate from deeper instincts, urges or drives.

Once you begin to conceive of humans as gregarious animals—motivated by self-preservation, food and sex, of course—you begin to understand a lot more about the tide of history. Trotter pointed out that a herd can achieve things that would be impossible for individuals (hunting in packs, running long distances—as wolves do—and so on). He felt that the instinct of gregariousness would manifest itself by an individual member of the group feeling good about doing things that serve the best interests of the herd and feeling uncomfortable about doing things that go against the herd's interests. In his view, the thoughts or feelings or desires that are derived from herd instincts would not be apparent to the individual at the time. A man in a group running from a predator wouldn't be thinking "I must do as the rest of the group are doing and run." He would simply feel uncomfortable if he did not run, and would feel comfortable if he ran. This point is important, because it is implied that the behaviour of the members of a group may be profoundly influenced by herd instinct, but that instinct would not reach the conscious level of—would not be "visible" to—the person at that instant.

It seems likely that several of our most readily adopted mindsets owe their origin to the so-called herd instinct, and I suggest that the common attitude that I call Them-and-Us-ing is one such example. When we get into an instant attitude of Them-and-Us, I suggest that in part we are often—in fact, usually—responding to signals that have triggered a herd instinct in us. That instinct is then manifested in the form of a change in the content of our thoughts (i.e., identification of Them, and conscious rationalization of the innate differences between Us and Them) and then, sometimes, action—for example, war.

This mindset—Them-and-Us-ing—is known to everybody and used by everybody every day. We can see it happening all the time at local, tribal, community and national levels, and we can see exactly the same process going on in our families and circles of friends.

It's all to do with recognition, with the way we identify and put value on certain features of other individuals and thereby decide that these are important factors in identifying those individuals as members of the same Us. We feel part of a group or a herd when these others have the same attributes that we do, and those attributes cover a vast range, from visible physical attributes to behavioural traits and all the way up to thoughts and beliefs. To put it in the form of a slogan: "If they *look* the same as we do, *behave* the same way we do, and *think* and *believe* the same way we do, then they are us," (or, more important, we are part of the same Us). Hence, group identity—commonality of appearance, behaviour, thought and belief—is the first essential component in turning a motley collection of individuals into a community (a much nicer word than Trotter's "herd").

So what are the mechanisms by which those individuals become—and stay—a cohesive unit? Presumably it can't be done solely by conscious thought or choice; presumably a hundred rabbits do not come together in a field and all individually think, "Hey! Here's an idea—why don't we all hang around together and start a warren?" Presumably herds are formed from individuals as a result of the instinct that Trotter called gregariousness, not as a result of individual decisions and choices. But how? What brings and holds the herd together? Of course that question is not (yet) fully answerable, but there are some clues about the ways a group or a herd keeps itself together. Perhaps these mechanisms could be termed (albeit rather inelegantly) "herd glues."

HERD GLUES

The first "glues" that hold communities together are the

immediately obvious physical attributes. Presumably rabbits (to stay with that example) recognize other rabbits as "rabbits like us" and do not start forming a herd with frogs or crows. At a slightly greater level of detail, they must also be able to recognize their own species, as opposed to other species of the same genus. Presumably cottontail rabbits can recognize other cottontails and do not start teaming up with jackrabbits.

Then, at a finer level of detail still, they must be able to identify with the *behaviour* (as opposed to the structure and the physical appearance) of other individuals. Clearly there are certain observable behavioural traits programmed into every species (by inbuilt instincts) that produce the same pattern of behaviour in individuals in response to species-specific signals. A famous example is the "danger" signal sent by the white underside of a rabbit's tail. When one rabbit finds itself in a dangerous position, it raises its tail (the technical word is "scut") and other members of the group run away. That is a behavioural reflex—an involuntary response to a stimulus. The inbuilt response of a rabbit to another rabbit's suddenly visible white tail has obvious evolutionary survival value to the species. It helps everyone who behaves that way.

Almost certainly there are equivalents of that in human behaviour. For example, it is likely that our instinctive reaction to the sight of blood is of the same type. When we see a viscous, sticky fluid that is coloured bright red and is distributed in drops or splashes or puddles (whether near a motionless human or not), I would imagine that our withdrawal response is involuntary (unless we are performing a surgical operation on a patient and have been trained to consciously override our instinctive withdrawal). These inbuilt responses that result in the same response by all members of the herd to the same stimulus are *behavioural* types of herd glue.

So, at the lower levels of detail, a herd is held together by the overall commonality of appearance, then at higher levels by the finer details of appearance and then at higher levels still by shared behavioural traits.

It is likely that future research will further define the role of other mechanisms contributing to this herd-bonding process—for example, chemical signals sent from one individual to other herd members. There is a family of chemicals called pheromones that are secreted in sweat in response to certain conditions. Pheromones are basically odourless hormones that work over a long distance and produce certain behavioural responses in the recipient. Some pheromones produce responses of aggression, some produce panic, others produce sexual attraction and courtship behaviour and so on. Many pheromones are probably species-specific and produce the appropriate behavioural response only if the recipient is of the same species as the emitter. This is why, I assume, a human doesn't share a rabbit's feeling of fright when the former startles the latter. Pheromones clearly play some role in holding a group together. They are known to be secreted by teenage girls at rock concerts, and they probably play a part in mass reactions at faith healings (where people faint by the dozen) and in other strong emotions shared by a crowd.

Although we are only beginning to understand the fine details of how pheromones work, it seems possible that they affect the limbic system (the inner parts of the temporal lobes that we discussed in Chapter 4). The amygdala is the only part of the brain that has a rich connection to the olfactory bulb, the area where signals from the nose are first received. This is still a bit speculative, but it is possible that pheromones—carrying "unsmellable" signals to the nose—send signals via the olfactory bulb to the amygdala and then produce changes in the person's behaviour by means of the limbic system. Whatever the final common pathway in the brain, pheromones assist in (or even create) patterns of behaviour that act as cohesive forces—herd glue—in a group.

At higher levels still, there are conscious and voluntary behaviour patterns that can act as signals of group membership and therefore as herd glues. These conscious and voluntary patterns of behaviour are still rewarded (in the Trotter sense of that word), in that the individual feels good about doing something that fits in with the best interests of the group. Hence, there is reward for an individual in carrying out conformist and imitative behaviour—doing what other members of the same group are doing, which includes mimicry.

This type of reward—perceived at a conscious, sapient level—is another factor in the creation of any unified activity, whether it is applause at a concert or a play, joining the army at the outbreak of a war, fighting as part of that army or any other group action or act of mimicry that one can think of. It might also be possible that this process of making a conscious decision or choice to fit in with the group is involved in smaller-scale activities, such as riots or lynch mobs. So thoughts or emotions at a conscious level—people thinking or feeling the same things as other people—may act in part as a herd glue.

Beyond this, there might be social rewards in imitating *insincerely*—behaving with a type of mimicry that conforms to the *group's* objectives, even though the *individual* doesn't genuinely feel it. Hence, we might see passive imitative behaviour—people "coming along for the ride" or behaving in ways that we label "acting out." This is a difficult area to discuss clearly, so let me offer some concrete examples. After the tragic death of Diana, Princess of Wales, there was a vast outpouring of emotion in Britain. Many thousands of people gave vent publicly to their grief. But there were some instances in which the response seemed to go beyond genuine or spontaneous expressions of emotion. For example, hundreds of people lined up to sign Diana's Book of Remembrance. A television crew interviewed and filmed people in that lineup. One woman said that she had just had a vision of Diana walking towards her and talking with her. When the crew asked others in the lineup, another woman said that she, too, had seen Diana. Both women were grieving, and, of course, visual hallucinations after bereavement are common. But here, there was obvious social pressure to produce a socially accepted phenomenon to order—a sophisticated and highly codified form of herd glue.

It is not possible to say whether the people who were interviewed really saw a vision of Diana (and it is almost impossible to say what the word "really" means in that context). Other examples abound. In many television interviews nowadays, for example, subjects feel pressure to cry while on camera. Sometimes this is clearly a spontaneous expression of genuine emotion, but in some cases it isn't. Subjects sometimes feel that crying is what is expected of them in discussing a particular topic, and they force themselves (sometimes unconvincingly) to cry during the interview. This is another example of behaviour that has questionable authenticity but is a genuine response to the individual's perception of what is socially expected and rewarded.

I think this is an important point, and one that is really worth stressing: social pressures may operate on the individual at a direct ("sincere") level and also at an imitative level of mimicry. It is likely that all these social forces originate in some way from the "instincts of the herd" that Trotter wrote about. Once rationalized and socialized, the final form of these instincts would feel to the individual just like any other voluntary or conscious action.

Of course, it is not possible to do justice to this complex subject in a few sentences, but the central observations are beyond dispute: humans are gregarious animals, and any group of gregarious animals is capable of achieving things that individual members are unable to do in isolation. This is why there is great survival value in the bonds that hold a group together and reward in behaving in conformity with the rest of the group.

Now let us look at one of the more important motivating forces that propels groups (and individuals) into action—aggression.

HERDS WITH ATTITUDE

The literature on the subject of animal behaviour (now known as the science of ethology) is vast, and I can claim to understand only the most popular books in the area, hoping that they are not merely populist but are academically sound as well.

The best starting point is Konrad Lorenz's book about aggression, called—logically enough—*On Aggression*. In it, Lorenz explains how aggression is actually a valuable mode of behaviour for a species and for a community. Most important, aggression helps groups of the same species to space themselves out across the environment to maximize the use of territory and the available food and water supplies. Aggression—in the sense that Lorenz and many subsequent ethologists use the word—is a basic trait that is common to most of the higher animals. Of that there is no doubt. But what happens to the aggressive ("gimme-some-space") instinct in modern humans? After all, most of us are not engaged in colonizing new places and do not have the option of moving into an uninhabited part of the country to utilize new food resources. So what happens to that aggressive instinct?

The answer is neither simple nor complete. Obviously the aggressive instinct is manifested in a wide variety of socialized forms, including all the body signals of aggression, such as snarling, baring of teeth and so on. But in addition, the concept put forward by Trotter is important: an individual may not recognize that some aspect of his or her behaviour is based on an instinct. We all know (mostly) when we are feeling angry and enraged—but at an earlier stage than that, how would we know if our feelings were based on an instinct of the herd? Although there is no firm proof at the moment, I would suggest that the fundamental stance of Them-and-Us-ing may often owe its existence to a group instinct of aggression, and may be built into the system, rather than originating as a conscious choice.

Lorenz restricted himself fairly closely to the observable features of animal behaviour, up to and including the primates. For some decades—really until the 1950s and 1960s—it was thought, or rather, hoped, that any conclusions drawn from animal behaviour applied to the "lower animals" only and had no relevance to human behaviour and human organization. Humans—so the doctrine went—were something altogether different, and extrapolation from other animal species was not legitimate.

It would have been much more comfortable for us as humans if that were true. It would have been *so* nice to think of our species as totally distinct from any other animal species, particularly when it comes to aggressive acts.

It would have been much pleasanter and easier for us to imagine that as sapient humans, we get involved in intergroup conflict only through rational and conscious decisions made using our higher powers of reasoning and thought. But over the last four decades or so, that notion has all but disappeared. Ethology has forced us to the conclusion that at least some (and probably many) traits of human behaviour may well be manifestations of underlying animal urges and instincts.

This is a tricky area. Making the comparison between animal behaviour and human behaviour has always been fraught with academic danger and is a difficult (but very popular) area of research and writing. Several books make creditable efforts at bridging the gap between animals and humans, and Robert Ardrey's *The Territorial Imperative* is one of the most interesting—though certainly a little idiosyncratic. Unlike Lorenz, and others such as Niko Tinbergen, who wrote as pure scientists of ethology, Ardrey felt free to extrapolate from the behaviour of animals (bees, birds, deer and many others) to human behaviour. He was trained as an anthropologist in the 1930s but later became a playwright. His facility with both scientific data and lyrical prose makes his writing a joy to read and seductively persuasive, even in fields where the data are somewhat thin. Even so, his opinions have survived in fairly large numbers.

Ardrey's main thesis is that much of animal behaviour is linked—by origin and by instinct—to the territory that the animal recognizes as its own. Animals have a sense of "home." There is a great deal of research in this area, and it clearly demonstrates that many species have innate behavioural patterns specifically related to, for example, their ability to navigate to a particular piece of turf that they recognize as home. In many species this is a fixed and vital part of their entire behaviour—and Ardrey suggests that humans are similar in that respect. Whether he is basically right (or basically wrong) about human territoriality is still a matter of considerable debate (and it's way beyond the borders of my own intellectual turf, anyway). But all the human concepts of home, homeland, possession of land, the concept of ownership in general and so on do certainly have features in common with observed traits in many animal species. We are clearly not exclusively and solely a territorial species, but it is equally clear that territory matters to us.

Which would probably not be a source of problems *if* there were enough habitable human territory to go round. Sadly, there isn't.

NO ROOM AT THE INN—OR ANYWHERE ELSE

So far, then, in our discussion of why humans gang up in groups and attack other groups, we have discussed the cohesive forces that hold groups or herds together and have looked briefly at the instinctive force of aggression.

Now we can ask why all this creates such a problem for humankind. After all, the human species is the only one that regularly slaughters millions of its own kind. Are there any inherent biological triggers contributing to that? The answer is that there are, and many biologists have pointed out the most important one: overpopulation. To put it simply, as a species we became too successful at colonizing this planet and filling up the apparently habitable areas of it. In fact, we became much, much, much, much, much, much, much (repeat the word one hundred thousand times if you want to give yourself the idea of the scale) too successful.

This area is, necessarily, a little speculative, but many biologists have looked at it, and at what happens in animal colonies (from mice to gorillas), and have attempted to draw parallels with human populations. One of the best-known writers on these biological traits underlying human behaviour is the zoologist Desmond Morris.

Morris has spent decades applying his zoologist-type observation skills to humans. His books have always been widely read and have, as a result, drawn some heavy fire from the more academic investigators. Yet, despite those criticisms, it is really worthwhile to consider some of his theories about the way patterns of animal behaviour may create problems in human community structures.

Morris, particularly in his book *The Human Zoo*, lays great emphasis on two aspects of human behaviour. First, we are a gregarious and co-operative species of animal—and we *are* a species of animal, not some race of alien beings entirely unrelated to the "lower creatures"; as such, we have many characteristics in common with "lower" species, even though we fondly imagine that we don't. Second, Morris emphasizes the fact that the human species has been outstandingly successful in colonizing all kinds of inhospitable environments, and as a result of that success, and the breeding practices that we have been able to sustain, our territory is now ludicrously overcrowded.

Just to put these things in perspective, when we speak about "ludicrous overcrowding," we don't mean merely, "Oh, isn't the traffic bad downtown during rush hour": we are talking about overcrowding by many orders of magnitude.

Morris speculates that a group of about sixty hominid apes might have been wandering about the savannah (doing their hunting-and-gathering thing) and roaming over an area of about a thousand square kilometres. (These figures are only approximate, but they give the idea.) If that were true, then in the "natural" state, humans would have over fifteen square kilometres per person.

At present, most of our species live at population densities 100,000 times more crowded than that—or even more. To give you some idea, the city of New York (near the upper end of the overcrowdedness scale) is about 775 square kilometres in area, and has a human population of about 7.4 million people. In the (postulated) natural state, instead of 7.4 million people, that land space would be home to perhaps a mere 46 humans (which would certainly reduce the strain on the subway system).

If those figures are an approximate guide, the world's population, which is currently about 6 billion, would actually be no more than about 40,000 (60,000 at the most).

That would make a difference, wouldn't it?

Morris suggests that many of the problems humans confront in daily life are the result of our biology. Our interpersonal communication systems (probably) evolved among a species of hunter-gatherer apes, and they are now being used by a species existing at unimaginable levels of complexity and overpopulation. No wonder we have so any problems—our wiring is terribly old-fashioned.

If we take Trotter, Lorenz and Morris (and a bit of Ardrey) together, a clear picture emerges. We are probably a gregarious herd-bound species held together by a variety of herd glues. In addition, we possess (in common with most animal species) a considerable amount of natural aggression, which in the distant past was useful in spacing out individuals across the environment. Unfortunately, we evolved a wide variety of extraordinarily successful behavioural traits that allowed us to multiply way beyond the "natural" (or, at least, expected) limits. As a result, we now find ourselves a herd filled with an excess of "gimme some space" aggression, in a situation without space to be given. The result is a constant turf war between our various herds within the herd. And as our species has become more and more sophisticated, so have our turf-defending instincts become more and more sophisticated, conscious and socialized in their expression.

As if all that were not bad enough, there are some other aspects of instinctive (or reflex) aggression that make things even worse.

MAKING THINGS WORSE: THROWING CAUTION TO THE WINDS

When we are under pressure—when our "blood is up"—we are not good at keeping a sense of perspective. In some wild corner of the savannah or veld this might be of considerable survival value; in the context of human society it is almost always a disaster. As we see every day in most aspects of our lives, humans seem to be particularly adept at losing all sense of perspective and proportion—often for very trivial reasons. We are all familiar with the sudden flood of rage over a small mistake in a shopping bill or purchase, or being cut off in traffic or other irritating everyday events. (By the way, the biology underlying this and many other aspects of human behaviour is beautifully incorporated into an overall account in Steven Pinker's book *How the Mind Works.)*

There are hundreds of millions of stories that illustrate this point, but one recent tragedy highlighted the phenomenon—in this case, "road rage." It happened on a highway in the United States. One woman felt that she had been cut off by another driver (also a woman), although police were later quoted as stating that there seemed to have been room for both vehicles on that stretch of road. The two drivers pulled over after several rude hand gestures and signals. One driver got out of her car and walked towards the other, who had a gun in her car and who shot and killed the first woman. It later turned out that the victim had been on her way to pick up her children: the woman who had just shot her made a call to the emergency services on her cell phone saying that she could not believe what she had just done.

Why do things like that happen? Why do we overreact in this way? Why did a man shoot his wife because his computer system crashed? Why do people shoot their neighbours over a dog that barks at night?

Part of the answer is in the way the fight-or-flight reflex or instinct is organized. In territorial disputes, once an animal starts to fight, in order to win it has to be able to suppress its own sense of pain, and probably its sense of danger as well. That is what the reflex is there to do. There are several mechanisms that assist in this, including functions of the autonomic nervous system, hormones such as adrenaline and other chemical compounds like endorphins. Endorphins are relatively simple chemicals secreted into the brain and the cerebro-spinal fluid around it that bind to pain receptors in the brain and by blocking them stop the individual from feeling pain. Mechanisms such as these play a major role in allowing an individual to go into a painful situation (such as a battle or a fire) and suppressing the usual response by "ignoring" or rather "not experiencing" the pain. In appropriate circumstances, mechanisms like these will allow the individual to be heroic and perform altruistic acts at great personal cost. The downside is that the same set of mechanisms also allows the person to ignore the normal curbs and limits to behaviour in some inappropriate circumstances—hence, I suggest, there occurs a loss of the sense of proportion, and catastrophes result.

Of course religious or spiritual beliefs are not implicated in incidents like these. All I am saying is that humans are primed to behave this way; the biology is set up to promote this kind of aggression and destruction. Road rage is an example of how easily the system is triggered, and other triggers can easily do the same. Religion can act as a trigger. It is not the fault of religion—in fact, if anything, it's the fault of our biological design combined with overpopulation—but it just happens that the human powder keg of aggression is easy to ignite, and religion is something that often and easily provides the right sort of spark.

"THIS IS A MATTER OF PRINCIPLE": RATIONALIZING AND AMPLIFYING

> Moral indignation is jealousy with a halo.
>
> —H. G. Wells (1866–1946)

RELIGIOUS ENDS AND EARTHLY MEANS

So, we appear to be a species that has inbuilt aggressive instincts, living at greatly excessive population densities and endowed with wonderful brains that can perform an activity called conscious thought.

The problem is that we sometimes use our wonderful brains to produce (among other things) rationales and reasons that seem (to us) to justify our instincts. This is sad because our rationalizing powers are enormous—as are our powers of aggression. Even sadder, our beliefs feed straight into this process. Because, by definition, beliefs are activities of the mind that cannot be proven or disproven by empirical fact, once a belief has been attached to an aggressive urge or act, it will stay attached and will go on amplifying it. It cannot be disproven because it is a belief.

Furthermore, there have always been certain segments of humankind who have lived by the axiom that the ends justify the means. This places religious beliefs in the best possible position to serve as a cause or as a promoter of aggression, for there can be no larger "ends" than the ultimate deity and eternal life.

It is a plain fact of human behaviour that many people become so attached to their own set of religious beliefs that they might be quite ready to die for them and—far more significant—to kill for them. The central rationale is not difficult to see—it is really a matter of how the believer weighs the costs compared with the benefits. To the earnest believer, the very considerable benefits associated with the goal (the ends) greatly outweigh the apparently trivial costs associated with the endeavour (the means).

Let me restate that point in plainer terms. If you have a sincere and fervent belief in one type of god, and if you are utterly certain that your god wants all humans to behave in a certain way and will punish you in the everlasting afterlife if you do not promote that view and will reward you if you do promote it, then you will feel that *anything* you do to achieve those ends is justified. The premium you pay is small compared with the perceived rewards. You might even die in your endeavour to make things happen the way your god has ordained—and you might well have to kill—but what is that, compared to the importance of achieving eternal reward? If the *ends* are really desirable, then even apparently horrendous *means* pale into insignificance by comparison. A horrific example of that in the nineteenth century was recorded by Frazer. He noted that in some tribes around the Bering Strait it was a custom, if the hunting was bad, for a hunter to kill a small child, dry the body and carry it in a bag. It was believed that this provided the hunter with the extra-sharp sight that young children were thought to have. We would feel horror and revulsion at the thought of the ends (i.e., feeding the rest of the community) justifying those means (the murder of an infant), but that community regarded it as unfortunate but necessary.

That is the way it has worked for centuries: if the ends are great enough, they justify the means. History is littered with trails of devastation caused when one group of people felt that it was justified in killing another for the sake of their concept of god and, sometimes paradoxically, in the name of the love for the rest of mankind that their god bade them stand for. The concept of the ends justifying the means seems to have been a prominent factor in rationalizing and justifying religious aggression. (I need to state once again—and emphatically—that religion is not the only *casus belli* that humans use. As a species, we have used almost every imaginable excuse as a justification for our inborn inter-herd aggressive instincts, including race, culture, language, politics and thousands of other conscious attributes. These can all be precipitating factors in starting conflicts—but it is important to note that religion has always featured very prominently in that list.)

Conflicts that have been started or perpetuated by religious violence make up an almost endless list. Here are just a few examples: the Crusades, the Spanish Inquisition, the persecution of the Huguenots, the Manichean schism, dozens of wars between Protestants and Catholics, between Muslims and Christians (Maluku in Indonesia is a present-day example), between Hindus and Muslims (for instance, in the partition of India) and civilian slaughter on religious grounds on the largest scale yet known, that of more than six million people, mostly Jews, in Hitler's Third Reich.

There are hundreds of other examples, but I want to pick just one in order to illustrate some of the barbaric actions that humans are capable of inflicting on other humans. It is a tiny and long-forgotten example from the sixteenth century, and it is valuable for two reasons. First, because history gives a perspective that reduces the pain very slightly and so might allow us to be a little more objective about the horror. Second, the barbarity is put into even sharper perspective because the outcome (the survival of the condemned group as an independent people) was regarded as totally inconceivable at the time by the Pope. Yet following the group's survival of several more massacres over the following century, their continued existence became accepted as a matter of course.[3]

In the sixteenth century, the Waldensians, a people of the Protestant religion living around Piedmont in the Austrian valleys of Valois, were condemned by the Pope. Here is an example of what soldiers of the Dukes of Piedmont and Savoy did to the Waldensians, as reported by a writer from that region:

3. The massacres in Piedmont continued for more than a century. John Milton (1608-1674) wrote a cry of outrage—"bloody Piedmontese, that roll'd mother with infant down the rocks"—in the poem "On the Late Massacre in Piedmont," which included a description in specific detail of the butchery.

There is no town in Piedmont where some of our brethren have not been put to death. Jordan Terbano was burnt alive at Susa; Hippolite Rossierso at Turin; Michael Goneto, an octogenarian, at Sarcene; Vilemin Ambrosio hanged on the Col di Meano; Hugo Chiambs of Fenestrelle, had his entrails torn from his living body at Turin; Peter Geymarali of Bobbio in like manner had his entrails taken out in Lucerna, and a fierce cat thrust in their place to torture him further; Maria Romano was buried alive at Rocca Patia; Magdelena Fauno underwent the same fate at San Giovanni; Susanna Michelini was bound hand and foot and left to perish of cold and hunger on the snow at Sarcena; Bartolomeo Fache, gashed with sabres, had the wounds filled up with quicklime, and perished thus in agony at Fenile; Daniel Michelini had his tongue torn out at Bobbo for having praised God; James Baridari perished covered with sulphurous matches which had been forced into his flesh under the nails, between the fingers, in the nostrils, in the lips and all over the body, and then lighted; Daniel Rovelli had his mouth filled with gunpowder which, being lighted, blew his head to pieces; Sara Rostignol was slit open from the legs to the bosom and left to perish on the road between

> Eyral and Lucerna; Anna Charbonnier was impaled and carried thus on a pike from San Giovanni to La Torre.[4]

What could have allowed the people who did these things to have slaughtered eighty-year-old men, to have tortured and murdered women and to have torn a man's tongue out for praising God? The same question can be asked of any act of destruction and barbarism. What allowed people to torture other humans on the rack or to crush them to death slowly under rocks? What allowed people to staff and organize Hitler's concentration camps and to kill and torture millions of humans predominantly because of their religion?

There are many components to the answer, and we have discussed some of the contributing factors already: first, the basic biological features such as herd instinct, natural aggression and response to gross overpopulation, which can all be amplified by secondary social factors, including the processes of rationalization. Among those, we can easily identify the justification of the means by the ends, a technique that is commonly called into play (at national and community levels) when events are already getting very heated. But even at "lower

4. This report was quoted by William James in *The Will to Believe* ("Is Life Worth Living?"), citing a book by George Waring about the Tyrol.

temperatures"—at ordinary, everyday levels of normal interpersonal conflict—there are significant processes of rationalization that we all commonly use to justify our various prejudices and animosities. I have coined a word to describe what I think is a very common one.

"MONSTRIFYING": THINKING IN BLACK AND WHITE

Part of the path to carrying out inhumane acts such as the ones I detailed above (events that we often flatter our species by calling "inhuman") is for the perpetrator to persuade himself or herself that the victim is somehow a lesser type of human being. In fact, it makes the perpetrated act even simpler for the perpetrator if he or she can think of the victim as not being human at all. A major part of that process of rationalizing is to try to think of the intended victim as *totally* worthless or evil. To do that, you first have to ignore the patchy mixture of right and wrong that we are all composed of—you have to persuade yourself that the intended victim is *entirely* "wrong" and has no "right" bits, all vice and no virtue.

The process of rationalizing the other person into a totally worthless object is the essential first step in sharpening the contrast between Us (whom we think of as good) and Them (whom we think of as bad). This is something that we all do, and it increases our tendency to enter into an escalating sequence of aggressive actions. At a personal level it usually doesn't matter very much—we have rows and arguments or contretemps and they mostly don't amount to much. Unfortunately, when communities, political groups, religions or entire countries do it, it fans the flames and might lead to such disastrous effects as war or genocide.

I call this thought process "monstrifying,"[5] and it is the act of thinking that a person (or a nation) is either totally good or totally bad, but cannot possibly be anything in between. When we monstrify, we seize on one or two aspects of a person's behaviour (or of a group's behaviour, or a nation's) and ignore everything else.

In marriages, this train of thinking leads to "theme arguments" ("You *always* do that . . . " "You *never* . . ." "You're *useless* because . . . "). In politics, it is a standard way of gaining ground on an opponent or on an opposing party ("You wouldn't want your president to be the kind of person who . . ."), implying that if someone has made a mistake in activity X, he must necessarily be useless/dangerous/untrustworthy in every activity from A to Z. In international affairs it's a major factor in racism, persecution, war and genocide.

5. By the way, I am using the word as the opposite of what has been called "demonstrifying"—a valuable technique in personal therapy. I owe Dr. Bernie Zilbergeld a debt for his having used the word in his book *The New Male Sexuality*.

The real problem with the act of monstrifying is that it is such a quick and easy solution to complex situations. When we monstrify, we can vent our anger and feel that we are quite justified in doing so ("Those dyed-in-the-wool bastards deserve exactly what's coming to them . . ."). We suppress the awareness of the features that we previously recognized and liked or even loved about the other person (because they are now inconvenient to our purpose) and we amplify in our own conception the features we dislike or disagree with.

A FEW AMPLIFYING FACTORS

Once a community is on the way towards a conflict, there are many conscious thought processes that can be recruited to amplify and augment it. These processes include misunderstanding of the other party's intentions, misjudgment of the other party's abilities or determination, simple (or complex) mistakes and so on. It is at this level that relatively small-scale disputes can inflate into enormous conflagrations. Perhaps the most significant example of this is the First World War. Although the causes of the First World War are legion, there is no doubt that both of the initiating powers (Kaiser Wilhelm's Germany and Czar Nicholas's Russia) sincerely believed that once a war was started, it would be resolved in a few months and at a relatively low cost to human life. In the end, as we all know, those estimates were wrong by more than four years and by nearly nine million soldiers and seven million civilians.

As pointed out by Wilfred Trotter (and by many other authors writing after him), the instincts of the herd (i.e., group dynamics or crowd behaviour) can readily become recruited into a conflict. All the attendant social values rewarding the behaviour that the group approves of—acts of heroism, following and exalting leaders, demonstrating altruism, courage, co-operation and so on—all of these come into play and might serve to recruit more members of the group into a conflict. As Trotter suggested (and as I think we all know) it feels good when we are doing things that are valued by the community. It is usually extremely difficult to resist these types of community pressures. Marching to the beat of a different drummer has never been easy.

MORTALS ON EARTH: TENANTS OR OWNER-OCCUPIERS?

Religion—as opposed to other precipitating factors such as politics or culture—has additional features adding momentum to its contribution to aggression. The concept of an afterlife is not only a promise of "gold at the end of the rainbow," it also changes attitudes to daily life.

If you happen to believe that there is an eternal

afterlife, then your view of mortal existence—and of the planet where mortals carry out that existence—may be changed. If you believe that the "real" life is in heaven after you have died, then you may (and many people do) regard life on earth as temporary. This is a potential source of problems.

The whole idea of the temporary or ephemeral nature of human life (compared with the eternity that follows it) has had a dramatic effect on our attitudes to our own lives and those of our fellows. Perhaps a good analogy is the difference between someone who owns his or her own home—an owner-occupier—and the tenant who simply rents the living space on a temporary basis. When you own your house, you take its problems seriously and personally. You are prodded (usually) into making minor repairs before they get worse, to prevent major damage from ruining your investment. But if you are the tenant, and if you think that your lease will expire before any major consequences will result, you may make a phone call or two to the owner-landlord, but you won't get too upset if a small leak wasn't fixed and if you have no investment to lose.

Of course not all people with a belief in the hereafter view their lives as being nothing more than temporary, and not every believer in heaven will totally ignore the day-to-day affairs of the world. But even so, the thought lurks in the background: if you think that your existence is merely a temporary occupancy of someone else's (i.e., god's) planet, your interest in the long-term consequences of your actions may be much less.

This feature of the believer's world-view is also amplified by the current atmosphere concerning personal responsibility. At present, particularly in the United States, large numbers of legal cases are bringing the question of responsibility to the courts. I am not saying that this is necessarily a bad thing in itself, but it is changing social attitudes. If a corporation sells you a cup of coffee, you do not have to assume that the coffee is hot unless the cup says so (this, following the result of litigation). Of course it is a good idea to warn the buyer, but there is an additional message: "You have no responsibility unless you have been given a specific warning." In my more gloomy moments, I wonder whether there will soon be a law requiring every dinner fork to bear an engraved warning stating: "This fork may cause blindness if pushed into your eye."

The fact that this process is going on in the courts all the time has an effect on our own expectations of ourselves and each other. I suggest that the general atmosphere of not-my-fault-ism is pervasive, and that it also has an effect on the way some people believe in a deity and expect things from that deity. As it becomes easier to blame someone else for injury incurred while driving your car with a cup of hot coffee between your knees, so it becomes easier to question what you, as an individual, are actually responsible for. This is a vast and active area of discussion, and I cannot presume to offer any answers. People are wondering how much of what they do wrong is their own fault, and how much can be blamed on some other party. Not-my-fault-ism can affect the way many of us respond to the crises around us.

THE LIVING HELL OF THE IDEA OF HELL

If our attitude to heaven can affect the way we behave in our everyday lives, so can our attitude to hell.

I want to discuss hell very briefly, since it is to some extent a rather outmoded idea. The concept that there is a physical place wherein those who have sinned and transgressed in life are imprisoned and tortured for all eternity has held sway for a very long time. Of course we can now see it as a projection of all-too-human ideas of punishment and justice into the eternal realm, and we may (perhaps) be able to feel a tinge of regret for all those millions of people who died in the Middle Ages and centuries after over issues related to heaven, hell, sin and transgression.

But is the idea of hell truly dead? After all, we are now in the beginning of the twenty-first century, and in the

Catholic Church the Pope finally defined hell as a mental state (and not an actual place) only in the year 1999. So perhaps the idea of a hell has not been completely extinguished yet. And if the idea still has a little bit of currency with some people, then all I need to say is that it might still be a problem created by theism.[6]

SAINTS, SINNERS AND THE ALLURE OF JUSTIFICATION

The danger inherent in all this lies in our use of the concept of a deity as justification for aggressive behaviour. It has gone on for centuries, as we have discussed, and it has led, tragically often, to killing. Before we close this section, it is worth discussing the act of justification in a little more detail.

One of the greatest descriptions of the process of justifying actions by religion was written over 150 years ago, and it was a novel, not a psychological treatise. It was published in 1824 by a Scottish writer called James Hogg. Actually, I suspect that in his time Hogg was a bit of an odd duck. Most of his writings (at least the ones I've read) are rather mundane pieces of poetry and prose about the aspects of daily life in rural and urban Scotland. In fact, his sobriquet was "The Ettrick Shepherd,"

6. For reasons of space in this book, I am not going to spend more time on the discussion of hell. A really good, comprehensive and readable overview of the history of hell is *The Origin of Satan* by Elaine Pagels.

which might give you some idea. But in among all the rather run-of-the-mill stuff, he wrote an extraordinarily powerful novel, *The Confessions of a Justified Sinner.*

The plot would do very well for a Hollywood movie today: it details the rise and rather rapid fall of Robert Wringhim, the son of an ordinary (or so it seems) couple. His parents become utterly convinced that they have been chosen by God. God's choice is revealed to them in a vision, and from that moment on they become convinced that they can—literally—do no wrong. When Wringhim is about twelve, a further divine revelation informs his parents that he is now the newest member of this Chosen band. (James Hogg is quite dispassionate about this, and never remarks that the deity appears to have been exceptionally choosy in nominating this particular group of Chosen. Picky might be the word.)

From the moment of his being Chosen, Robert feels justified in whatever he does, and his life nose-dives. He moves rapidly down the scale of crime and depravity, justifying each of his selfish and destructive acts as the passionate actions of a saint trying to change the world. Eventually he kills his half brother. After that he has an epiphany in which he sees the error of his ways, and he commits suicide. (The manuscript where he documents all of the above is supposedly discovered many years later in his grave.)

I have no idea how *Confessions of a Justified Sinner* (or *The Private Memoirs and Confessions of a Fanatic*, as it was originally titled) was received at the time it was published. My guess is that it was regarded as very naughty, bordering on heretical, by the establishment, but it was probably never judged to be a genuine threat to organized religion (which it clearly wasn't). It was—as far as I can tell—the first novel to protest against the dangers of self-righteousness and religious superiority.

"I WOULD KILL IN GOD'S NAME": THAT TEMPORAL LOBE AGAIN

Now we come to some neuroscientific information that goes a long way towards explaining the close link between religious beliefs and aggressive behaviour—and it involves the temporal lobe and the limbic system (as we discussed in some detail in Chapter 4).

Since the very origin of organized societies, leaders have always claimed that their struggle was blessed by their god or gods. In fact, no leader has ever dared say the opposite. (As one wonderful lecturer recently put it, "No general has ever appeared in front of his army and said, 'I had a long talk with God in my tent last night, and he said this time he's going to side with the Turks.'" For Turks, you can substitute French or Austrians or any opponent of your choice.)

Every country, in every epoch, that ever went to battle has been convinced that god was on their side (although no side has ever commented on that after they have lost a war). However, there are some recent and important neuroscientific experiments that show that this god-is-on-our-side thought process might go much deeper than a convenient or popular sociological phenomenon: it might be due in part to the way the human brain is structured—particularly that all-important right temporal lobe.

As we discussed in Chapter 4, Michael Persinger is the neuroscientist who has investigated many features of the temporal lobes and their influence on behaviour. He used his carefully validated Personal Philosophy Inventory questionnaire on groups of university students over a period of fifteen years (from 1982 to 1996). Included in the PPI was item 136: "If God told me to kill, I would do it in his name"—a question requiring an answer yes or no. Among a total of 1,482 university students, 7 per cent answered yes.[7] Interestingly, that figure of 7 per cent was basically steady over the fifteen years; it didn't vary with the political or social climate. Furthermore—and this is just as important from the point of view of this chapter—

7. M.A. Persinger, "'I Would Kill in God's Name': Role of Sex, Weekly Church Attendance, Report of a Religious Experience and Limbic Activity," *Perceptual and Motor Skills* 85 (1997): 128–30.

the people who answered yes to the "kill in God's name" item were also much more likely than the average student to go to church weekly for most months of the year, to have had a religious experience that they believed was real and to have had Complex Partial Epileptic-Like experiences. Furthermore—perhaps not surprisingly—more of them were men.

Of course, one musn't jump to conclusions from these results. It is very interesting, nevertheless, that 7 per cent of average university students—approximately one in fourteen—would kill in God's name, and the students who would do this are in general more "religious" than average and have greater lability of the temporal lobes.

These experiments and observations suggest (but of course do not prove conclusively) that the human brain contains pathways that make it very easy to undergo religious experiences. Furthermore, this tendency has a demonstrated association with the self-perceived ability to perform aggressive acts (i.e., killing) if it appears that this is an order from a deity.

Persinger expresses the wider implications of these observations when he writes (perhaps a little sweepingly):

> Although wars may be driven by economic and political variables, the capacity to maintain the

> group dynamics is strongly determined by the manipulation of religious beliefs. Religious belief systems, which could be considered the social representation of normal individual egocentricism, encourage an association between personal immortality and the total validity of the culture's god. The discrimination of signs particularly if they are paired with religious beliefs can be and have been interpreted as justifications for killing other human beings during periods of economic or social uncertainty.

This is of course a science in its infancy. We simply do not yet have the scientific data—or even the vocabulary—to make more definitive or conclusive statements, so we cannot go any further along that path at the moment, but these early results are significant and genuinely thought-provoking.

SUMMARY: HOW STORM CLOUDS GATHER

Humans are community-based, gregarious animals, endowed with natural aggression but also conscious thought and great powers of collaboration and cooperation. Like all herds, human herds depend on a variety of signals to keep them together—including, at the higher levels, their conscious thoughts and beliefs. These can provide momentum or precipitating causes for aggression leading to destructive conflict when one subgroup—a herd within a herd—distinguishes itself from another on the basis of race, culture, religion, politics or any other of dozens of possible reasons. Once started on that road, the group then uses rationalization and conscious thoughts and attitudes to amplify the growing conflict.

That chain of processes could accurately be called the "biological-rationalizing cascade," and it is one way of conceptualizing the way that conflicts and wars develop.

The diagram that follows shows how these processes can be seen as linking together to lead from the normal and useful animal "gimme space" aggression to destructive conflict.

To recap what I am saying about the role of religious differences: in the process of rationalizing these instincts, all kinds of differences may be employed—but religious differences (because the desired "ends" can be seen as vastly more significant than the "means") are particularly well placed. To put it simply, every group can find things about itself that set it apart from other groups (from skin colour to fashion accessories), but religious differences—and I hope this doesn't sound like a cutesy slogan—are different from other differences. They are potentially more dangerous; they have a higher potential for causing explosions.

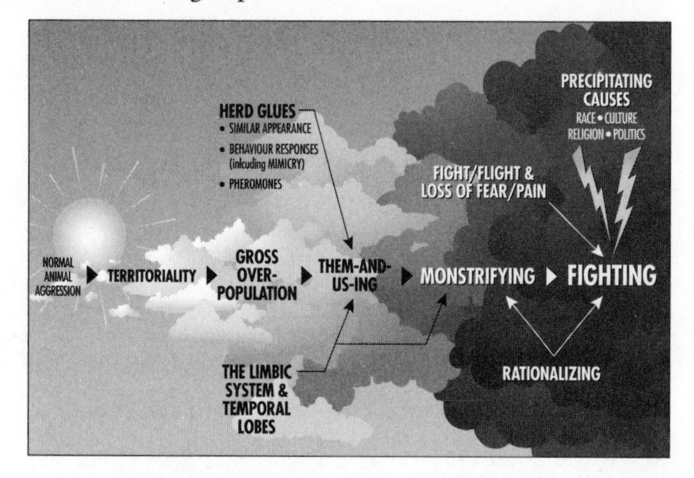

People differ about all sorts of ideas, and these differences frequently lead to violence—conflicts about political ideas are a good example. But in many other areas of thoughts and ideas, we can accept a difference of opinion without it escalating to lethal behaviour. In science, as far as I know, no group of people has ever been massacred because they believed in phlogiston, for example (or didn't), or believed in the inheritance of acquired characteristics or some other erroneous cul-de-sac of scientific theory. It is true that Galileo was punished (by the burning of his books and of the hand that wrote them) because he believed that the earth moved round the sun and not vice versa. But he wasn't punished by a group of scientists who disagreed with his hypothesis, he was punished by the Catholic Church. (Interestingly, as he put his hand—as ordered—into the flames, he is reputed to have muttered "*E puor se muove.*" ["Even so, it moves."] He was referring to the planet earth, and of course he was right.)

By and large, though, disputes about scientific ideas—ideologies, even—among scientists do not lead to violence and wars. They lead to letters in journals, publications, debates and on occasion even best-selling books about diets or aliens or longevity and millions of dollars in royalties—but rarely (if ever) do they end in physical aggression. Religious beliefs—which may be just as fervent—often do lead to physical aggression, and in this chapter we've looked at some of the reasons for that, including the I-would-kill-in-God's-name propensity inherent in some people's right temporal lobes.

Of course this cannot be definitively proven—it's just a hypothesis. But as I said at the beginning of the chapter, if you happened to be an anthropologist viewing this planet from another solar system, that hypothesis would fit the data quite well.

CHAPTER SEVEN

Being Good—Some Alternative Principles

A CONSIDERATION OF CONSIDERATION

In Chapter 6, we looked at some of the destructive things that humans do when they feel that they can justify their aggressive urges on the basis of a theist belief. We do not need to belabour that point further—we can all recognize and identify what is "bad" when it happens, whether it is justified on grounds of politics, religion, territory, power or just plain greed. That's what much of the human species (on good and altruistic days) would like to avoid. Now we need to think about the criteria by which we can identify something as "good."

If you happen to believe that the codes of good behaviour (i.e., proper, moral, ethical and decent conduct) have not been set in stone by a deity and do not come down to us from above, what then? What *can* you believe, and what rules can you abide by if they are not god-given?

There are, of course, many answers. Non-theists, individually and in groups, have their own ways of expressing their beliefs and the fundamental principles for which they stand. As one example, the group I belong to (and I'm currently president of a national organization) is the Humanists, and together we have produced a distillation of non-theist principles. These principles express a code of beliefs that can form a basis for reasonable behaviour, one that is not handed down from a deity but is based on the way humans behave.

Like any principles, they are useless if they are ignored. But at the very least they are a set of accessible, identifiable and discussible criteria by which we may distinguish constructive, ethical and good activity from bad and destructive acts.

As you will see, these principles are entirely related to the strengths and weaknesses of human behaviour, the main idea being to reinforce the former and discourage the latter.

At first glance, you will see that there is a good deal in common between these core beliefs and some of the central principles of many of the religions of the world. Among these areas of overlap, the most important is consideration or awareness of the consequences of one's actions. Superficially, that might appear to be simply a restatement of the Golden Rule (treat others as you would like to be treated yourself), but there is a very significant difference, as I will later explain.

Perhaps the most important thing to bear in mind about these principles is that they do not have their foundation in revelation or dogma. They are more to do with "this is the way we are" than a proclamation of "this is the way god ordained us to be."

As you read the set of principles that follows, I'd like you to ask yourself whether you can argue with or dispute their implications for human behaviour. If, at the end of the list, you find yourself thinking, "Well, they seem pretty good—people who behave in accordance with these beliefs would be quite decent people," then in a way you have answered for yourself the question in the title of this book. If you can imagine people sticking to these beliefs, and if you would find such people good, you are at the point of recognizing that human behaviour *can be* good without god.

SOME NON-THEIST CORE PRINCIPLES

1. The human species has evolved as—and remains as—part of nature.

Humankind is no more than—and no less than—a part of

nature: like all living organisms, humans have a life that is limited in duration and scope.

2. Human consciousness is a function of the activity of the human brain.

Being aware of the rest of nature—and of the universe—and of its own place within it is a characteristic of humankind's mental functioning that is perhaps unique and certainly wonderful. Nevertheless, consciousness is another aspect of natural life, and not a force or essence instilled into humans by an outside deity or intelligence. An individual's consciousness ends when that person dies.

3. Human beings require (to some extent) a system of belief in order to function.

So far, most belief systems have revolved around the idea of an external god or gods; however, the same need to believe can be equally served by alternative systems of philosophy. The Humanists' system is founded on using the scientific method to establish the factual basis of any data, and on basing human behaviour on reasonable conduct and democratic principles.

4. Humanists believe that in all its forms the supernatural is a myth.

Believing in an external God is a uniquely human activity.

While it has undoubtedly produced some advantages for humankind, it has also been a source of considerable divisiveness and strife. Humanists are people who do not believe in the idea of a Divine Architect or Regulator who has constructed the universe and controls human affairs, and they reject religions based on dogma, revelation or mysticism.

5. The human species is capable of achieving a great deal using its resources of collaboration and creativity. The results of these endeavours often benefit our species and planet, but we are also capable of using the same abilities in acts of destruction and cruelty.
The human species has always carried out acts of great benefit, but also acts of great destruction. Humanists recognize that the human species is innately capable of both of these—and that the potential for destruction is part of the human repertoire. Acts of mass aggression, killing and war are a result of tendencies built into human behavior and are not simply the result of a few abnormal and aberrant individuals. As a species we can clearly do many good things, but we need to be aware that we are capable of the opposite.

6. Humanists do not believe that the rules of human conduct have been set or preordained by any deity or external intelligence.
Clearly, no single religion has been able to show that it

has exclusive access to the secret of peaceful and co-operative co-existence of life on earth. There is much merit in the idea that there is no such thing as an extrinsic set of rules imposed on us from outside humankind that should be governing all of human behaviour.

7. Individuals who are aware of the consequences of their actions on other individuals, on the community and on the species are likely to behave in a more considerate, more reasonable and more ethical way.
Striving for the greater good and worth of the human species is not an exclusive property of theism. It is a human activity that can exist just as well without a belief in a deity as it can with it. Non-theists can be—and often are—ethical and moral people.

8. Humanists believe that equality of opportunity is a fundamental principle on which humankind can base its behaviour.
Equality of opportunity should be supported for all people, no matter what their nation, ethnic background, gender, sexual orientation or any aspect of their beliefs.

9. Life on earth is relatively fragile and requires care and attention to continue.
There is nothing guaranteeing our species against all

causes of potential extinction. Our own activities may threaten our existence, and we need to be aware of this in organizing and regulating what we do.

10. Humankind's destiny is not predetermined—much of it lies in our own control.
There is hope. But it's up to us to look after each other and ourselves.

Appendix: Here's one additional guideline—not a core belief, just a suggestion: if you have children, do your best to like them.
Much of humankind's woes seem to stem from children abused and disliked by their parents or caregivers as they grew up. The world will not be perfect if every child is not only loved but also liked, but it will probably be a lot more stable.

CONSEQUENCES VERSUS EXPECTATIONS

Now that you've looked over these basic principles, I would like to return to the issue of consideration, and to discuss the ways in which that principle (paragraph 7 in the above list) differs from the Golden Rule—which, as we have noted, is a principle shared by most religions and many non-theist groups.

There is an important difference between, on the one hand, treating others as you would want to be treated yourself and, on the other, trying to be aware of the consequences of your actions on others. The difference is that under the Golden Rule you project your *own* expectations onto the other person. If, on the other hand, you are guided by the principle of consideration of consequences, then you will try to anticipate the resulting effect on the other person (ignoring, if need be, the way you would respond if it were you). That is a difference worth noting.

A basic feature of human life is that all of us have suffered slights and insults (even abuse) in the past, and we all have a tendency to regard our past experience as a justification for doing the same to other people ("the wheel continues to turn"). Our expectations are—subconsciously and consciously—coloured by the kind of treatment we have received. And that (unfortunately) provides us with a ready justification for aggressive and destructive behaviour. In other words, we all have a tendency to behave aggressively—it's an instinct—and then to justify it by saying to ourselves that this is what we ourselves would expect if we were at the receiving end.

As you read this, you know, of course, that I am describing a simple fact of life: justifying a selfish act on the basis of our own expectations is something we all do from time to time. For example, we see it every day in the way that people drive on the highway! We all have a tendency—which is sometimes very prominent and is sometimes (on our better days) less prominent—to be competitive and aggressive, to be selfish. That is a fact of human behaviour, and we cannot pretend that this tendency does not exist. All we can do is to try to correct for it (if possible) and stop it from dominating and controlling our behaviour.

The Golden Rule (if anybody actually paid attention to it in everyday life) might go some of the way to accomplishing that, but it has a serious flaw. The flaw in the Golden Rule is that it can be used so easily as a justification for selfish instincts—it is just as likely to feed into our aggressive instincts as it is to promote more constructive behaviour. ("Of course it was reasonable for me to cut off that inattentive driver—*I'd* expect to be cut off if I were just bumbling along as *he* was.")

The principle of being aware of the consequences is less likely to have that effect. If you do stop and think about the effect of what you are about to do on the people you are about to do it to, you might reconsider a potentially destructive act.

SUMMARY: JUST IMAGINE . . .

Once again, my repeated disclaimer: the central point of this whole book is not whether god does or does not exist. The real issue is whether it would be a better world if we all *imagined* that god did *not* exist and if we behaved in accordance with that possibility, trying to sort out our own messes and trying to create our own solutions.

This, of course, might not be easy: but try to think about it in a different way for a moment. I would like you to take a big deep breath (in your mind) and try to imagine something that, for a minute or so, may seem rather frightening to some people. Try to imagine that we humans—and all other life forms on this planet—are here as a result of pure random chance.

Let's assume that everything we know about the origin of the universe from scientific observation so far is correct. Imagine that there was a big bang that created the universe, and that billions of stars formed from condensations of matter. Out of those billions of stars, one yellowish one, in a spiral galaxy, ended up with nine planets revolving around it. The third-closest of those just happened to have a compound of hydrogen and oxygen called water, and, after a few billion years, carbon-based life originated in that water. After a long time, some of that life evolved into oxygen-breathing land-dwelling forms, and some of those then developed backbones, then warm-bloodedness and later on (*much* later on) erect posture and opposable thumbs. Some of those erect warm-blooded animals then developed brains that were far more complex than those of any other living creature. One of the things that a complicated brain could do was to create what seemed to be a very sophisticated communicating and signalling system—language—which enabled its owners to transmit their thoughts to others of the same species. It was therefore a vehicle by which new ideas could be spread and transmitted to the whole species. Using that vehicle of ideas—plus a whole lot of other biological mechanisms—that species (now self-styled "humankind") populated the planet, and thought about itself and about its home, Earth.

Now imagine that the whole process I have just described was genuinely and totally random, without an external intelligence creating and regulating it. Is it not possible that given the length of time the universe has existed, randomness (without divine guidance) could have created exactly what we see around us today? I think you will have to admit that it is at least possible.

At this moment in the history of our planet, we know a bit about it and a bit about us. Unfortunately, we are still a rather superstitious, myth-hugging species; we are easily frightened and fearful of the unknown. Furthermore, our brains are hard-wired in such a way that we are easily tipped into experiencing divine or spiritual interpretations of things that we see or feel. We are built that way. We have a predilection for seeing the hand of an external deity in the turn of events. We tend not to see the world as the result of chance, but as part of the design of a celestial architect, a god who acts, at the very least, as a Prime Mover. In many ways, this supposition has been beneficial to our species, but in many other ways it has been a precipitating factor in strife and acts of destruction.

It doesn't have to stay that way indefinitely. We do not have to be totally imprisoned by our biology. If occasionally we can see ourselves in a cosmic context—as a carbon-based life form possessing language on the third planet around an average yellow star—there is room for improvement. As a species, we could do a lot better for ourselves by trying to imagine that it is up to us to sort out our own problems instead of waiting for some external intelligence to do it for us.

To express this concept in nutshell form (suitable for an extra-large T-shirt or bumper sticker): **the world will be a better place if we all *believe* whatever we wish, but *behave* as if there is no deity to sort out humankind's problems.**

Which leads me—logically enough—to a simple question: How do you do that? How do you behave as constructively as possible, no matter what you believe? The next chapter will offer some answers and options that may help.

CHAPTER EIGHT

In Thought, Word and Particularly Deed

PRACTICAL STEPS: OUTLOOK AND INSIGHT

Right now you are probably thinking along these lines: "Okay, this all sounds fine, but how does it happen?" How do you carry any of this into real life—how can you tap into any of this stuff to change behaviour?

The answer might sound easy, although, in practice, it is quite labour-intensive: you need insight in your outlook.

Building insight into your everyday problem solving and emotion handling is quite an art. It is also a very popular subject for authors of self-help books—there are hundreds about acquiring and using insight in your own motivation, and gaining control of your own emotions. I cannot claim to have read all of them (life is too short) but I have read some, and by and large they say sensible things, and make points about human frailties that are virtually unarguable. The greatest challenge for ordinary individuals like you and me lies in putting these principles into action.

The good news is that there are several books that are quite practical. One that I have found very useful is called *The Dance of Anger*, written by psychologist Harriet Lerner. The book is primarily directed at dealing with anger, but the same techniques can be of great value in dealing with all other major emotions, such as anxiety, disappointment, sadness, depression and so on. What makes it such a useful book is that there is no pretence that we "shouldn't" feel the anger (or any other strong emotion) that we all experience from time to time. Lerner basically encourages us to use our anger as a *guide* to identify the issue that is upsetting us, and then to look at that issue and explain it in as constructive and dispassionate a way as possible. (In the language of communication skills, this process of acknowledgment is called an empathic response, and it is important when you feel angry to carry out an empathic response to your own emotion.)[1] Lerner gives many examples of how you might "look" at your own feelings of anger—with

1. I teach communication skills to medical students—and in the basic language of communication skills, recognizing and then exploring an emotion in a dispassionate way is best achieved using something called an "empathic response." This consists of three steps: (a) identify the emotion; (b) identify the source or cause of the emotion; and (c) respond in a way that shows you have made the connection between (a) and (b).

parents, spouses, siblings, colleagues and so on. Instead of merely exploding in a sudden rage, you try to be as constructive as possible as you *describe* your emotion to the other person. In a nutshell, it means *explaining* your anger, rather than simply *exhibiting* it, *describing* it rather than *displaying* it. It makes a very big difference to the dialogue. Usually it steers the discussion away from escalation and confrontation and moves it onto a track that can (with perseverance) lead to resolution.

Now, there is an important step to take before you apply the empathic response to yourself. You have to *realize* that you are angry—in other words, you have to *acknowledge* to yourself that you are feeling angry. Again, there are lots of self-help book that discuss this particular issue (parts of Richard Carlson's *Don't Sweat the Small Stuff* are very good, as is Daniel P. Goleman's *Emotional Intelligence*). The key here is to recognize your own feelings as they arise; you have to know the signs in yourself of anger or rage or anxiety or sadness. This means that when you have experienced a flood of emotion you should try to say to yourself, "I've just been *really* angry—let me remember what it felt like, so I recognize it at an earlier stage next time." This process of gaining insight into one's emotions was probably what was meant by the famous ancient Greek maxim γνοθη σε αυτον (know thyself). This was reputed to be the most important advice ever given by the oracle at Delphi, and it became a favourite maxim of the Greek philosopher Socrates of Athens in the fifth century BC. If he had written a book it would have sold billions!

The two key steps in "knowing thyself" are (a) acknowledgment—which means knowing yourself and your emotions and recognizing that you are beginning to experience an emotion, and (b) responding in as constructive and dispassionate a way as possible in order to deal with the root cause. Although this is very easy to say and to visualize while we are feeling calm, it is of course extremely difficult when our blood is up and we are riding an emotional tidal wave.

There is perhaps one anecdote that is worth passing on about the difficulty of identifying and locating a deep-seated emotion or a feeling within oneself. It is said that a Confucian scholar once approached the twenty-eighth Buddhist patriarch, Bodhidharma, and asked for help "to pacify my soul." Bodhidharma's answer was quite simple: "Produce it and I will pacify it." The Confucian scholar was (in my view) extremely honest: "That's the trouble," he said, "I cannot find it." To which Bodhidharma replied: "Your wish is granted." And the Confucian scholar left in peace.[2]

Acknowledging that you can't get the answer is often the best way of dealing with a difficult question.

2. Quoted in Joseph Campbell, *The Hero with a Thousand Faces*, from Chapter 2: "Initiation."

PUTTING SPACE BETWEEN BELIEVING AND BEHAVING

What we have been talking about here is simply the technique of using our conscious thought processes to try to recognize and compensate for our own destructive instincts—preferably before we have done anything too destructive. Naturally, this process often fails in everyday life. We regularly give vent to anger or anxiety or disappointment, by which we mean that the emotion is translated directly into action. The feeling determines the behaviour—even against our wishes. We are often unable to interject some conscious and voluntary decisions *after* the emotion and *before* the action. It is obvious that this would be a better world if all of us attempted (at least) to interpose some measure of introspection—insight—between the emotion and its implementation. Acknowledgment of the emotion is the first part of that: being aware of one's feelings at least gives one's conscious and rational processes a chance to correct for potentially destructive activity.

Now I must not get too neuroscientific about this, because we don't have sufficient data yet to make firm conclusions or statements. But *if* it is true—as seems likely—that our emotions involve various parts of our brain's limbic system, including the deeper parts of the temporal lobes, then (in very crude terms) what one is doing could perhaps be expressed in neurological terms. At that moment of introspection, while applying an empathic response to one's own emotional state, one is trying to use conscious processes (which originate in the higher parts of the brain, the neocortex) to diminish the effect of the limbic system. I like to call that "using your neocortical brakes to try and slow down your limbic motor." That might not (yet) be a proven fact of neuroscience, but it sure helps to understand things in the meantime.

This section has been a scandalously brief overview of what is, after all, one of the most popular topics in the whole of human behaviour (apart from sex), but it would extend the mandate of this book too far to go into further detail or to spend longer discussing it. Therefore, I would simply like to reiterate that all the "good" principles in the world won't help you (or anyone else) unless you are able to enhance your ability to act with some consideration of the consequences.

ARE YOU A THEIST OR NOT? HOW TO MAKE THE DIAGNOSIS

Finally, we come to a sort of crunch. In all our discussion so far, we have been looking at the effects of belief in an external deity on the behaviour of the individual. So now I want you to ask yourself whether you hold such a belief or not.

We have discussed the origins and functions of belief, some of the detrimental aspects of human behaviour amplified by belief in an external deity and a set of principles and guidelines for "good" behaviour that do not have a god figure at the centre. So now it might be valuable to ask yourself that important question, Are you personally a believer in an external deity (a divine architect and controller) or not?

In view of everything we have been discussing, the difference between a theist and a non-theist might seem blurred. After all, if a person performs something that she or he calls meditation, and another person does exactly the same thing (as far as they both can establish when they discuss it) but calls that same action "prayer," is there a difference between the two people?

This is not a trivial matter, or simply a matter of wordplay. Over the course of human history this difference has been crucial. As we saw in Chapter 6, from a historical viewpoint the most destructive aspects of religious fervour come to the surface when people use their belief in an external deity to justify aggression and destruction. So, does an external deity exist for you?

I would like to propose a type of diagnostic test. If

you think about the following question, it will be clear to you whether your acts of prayer or meditation (or whatever name you choose) depend on an external deity or on an internal, personal religion (which I chose to call spirituality in the introduction of this book).

The test question is this: When you pray or meditate or seek strength or try to work out what to do about a big problem in your life, what do you do?

Whether you go to a church or any other place of worship, whether you are alone or in the company of others doesn't matter. Here's the crucial point: where do you feel you are (mentally) looking to get your guidance and strength? Where do you think the source is? If you feel that you are looking outward and upward towards the source, you are a believer in an external deity. If you look inward for your inspiration and strength—no matter what you call that source of strength (be it god, conscience, spirituality, essence, soul or any other name)—you are a non-theist. Other groups with this second type of belief system call themselves variously Humanists, agnostics, freethinkers and atheists.

The difference is therefore a fundamental one: do you believe that the source of the indefinable, ineffable essence that might improve, enlighten and elevate you is located inside you or outside you? I would like to suggest that people who believe the essence is inside are a bit less likely (perhaps a lot less likely) to start a religious war and destroy other human beings for the sake of that essence.

I am going to leave that question—and its answer—with you for the moment, and conclude this chapter by setting out the two types of answers (the theist and the non-theist reponses) to a commonly asked question. It is asked whenever any alternative codes of behaviour are discussed: Why *should* anyone behave decently, anyway?

SUMMARY: "WHY SHOULD I?"

The question, Why *should* I behave decently? is almost always raised during discussions about codes of behaviour, with an implied warning contained within it, namely, What's going to make someone go along with the code if they don't want to?

For people who believe in an external deity that has absolute power of reward and punishment the answer is simple: God will reward you if you do right, and will punish you if you do wrong. That answer is, of course, unarguable. Nobody has come back from heaven or hell to vouch for the truth of this claim, so it remains now, as it always has been, an act of faith.

Non-theists have more thinking and explaining to do. For non-theists, the human race is a large, variegated herd that can either make life easier for its members or more difficult. And so the answer to the question, Why should I? is Because it will be a better world for the human race if we all do.

When you come to think about it, even if the phrase "better world" sounds a little vague, it does reflect the way that civilization has advanced over the last few millennia. Throughout history, the rise of a race or a people has followed roughly the same course. One group achieves prominence and dominance over others by force of arms and initially maintains that superiority by direct physical control. Then after a time—and it might be decades or more, usually centuries—they gradually stop dominating others by pure brute force. I have always assumed that the Visigoths or the Vikings—or the ancient Romans, for that matter—gradually used less and less force in controlling their empire, and tried to maintain their own world order by using rules and laws. Presumably the Visigoths *could* have continued to use pillage and rape as a system of government, but on balance decided not to. The move towards the rule of law must have been a choice, a conscious decision (albeit a slow and gradual one).

So civilization can be seen as a process that arose because humans preferred it to simple force. Humans have become as civilized as they are because, deep down, we all feel that civilization is a better system than brutish dominance. It requires less maintenance. It is a "better world" if different peoples can agree on a set of rules, limits and frontiers and do not simply grab whatever they can when they can. A civilized "better world" requires less maintenance than a "grab what you can" one.

At first sight, that might seem a rather grey and wishy-washy answer (particularly when compared with a simple, thunderous demagogic answer such as, You should be good because God says so—and he says so through me, sinner!). Even if it is less colourful, the non-theist answer is still the only really constructive (and hopeful) one.

CONCLUSION

What If Life Is Merely a Sexually Transmitted Terminal Disease?

IS LIFE MEANINGLESS IF YOU ARE A NON-THEIST?

No.

Life is not pointless if there is no external deity any more than *any* human activity that requires effort, doggedness and concentration (chess, hockey, educating children, poetry, marriage, cooking, doing the crossword, to name but a few) is meaningless. None of these has any *intrinsic* meaning. Undoubtedly there are people somewhere who might believe that one of these activities is totally meaningless and pointless while at the same time being utterly devoted to another of them. The meaning of life—like the meaning of any human activity—lies in what you bring to it.

Here's an analogy: to some people, hockey is a metaphor for all human endeavour, heroism and magnificence; to many more it is an exciting and thrilling spectacle; and to a few heretics and eccentrics, hockey is just-a-bunch-of-guys-with-sticks-chasing-a-black-block-along-some-ice. There is no "correct" answer—the meaning of hockey is not an absolute quantity established or preordained outside the realm of human activity. The meaning of hockey is no more and no less than the meaning that the participants and the spectators imbue it with. The same is true of every endeavour. It is up to you.

And what applies to perceived meaning in life also applies to the perception of god in life. That, also, is a choice. For many people, the meaning of life is not apparent to them unless they can see god in every aspect. For many others, there is no such necessity. Belief in god may be an absolutely essential prerequisite for finding meaning in life—or it may be entirely unnecessary.

Whether you believe in god or not, however, it does seem that the act of believing is in itself necessary to humans. The activity of believing (of holding some consistent attitudes towards the world extending beyond available facts) is an essential feature of human life.

Non-theists (myself included) hold a large collection of other beliefs: beliefs that add up to a set of values (as described in Chapter 7). To express it as a slogan: "The facts of human life are one thing—what you make of them depends on you." The "what you make of it all" activity partly depends on the things you believe in and on the emotions you feel.

Even though I come at this from a direction diametrically opposed to that of William James, he expressed it beautifully when he wrote, "Believe that life *is* worth living, and your belief will help create the fact."

WHEN BAD THINGS HAPPEN

I would like to extend this discussion about meaning into one further area: the meaning of suffering. Over the centuries, many thousands of theist writers have stated or implied that it is virtually impossible to face catastrophes and disasters if you do not have a belief in a divine plan and faith in the ultimate justice and wisdom of a divine creator and controller. I would like to propose an alternative viewpoint: that you can face up to and deal with catastrophe without believing in a deity or a divine plan. That viewpoint was encapsulated in the best book by far on this subject, Viktor Frankl's *Man's Search for Meaning*.

Viktor Frankl was an extraordinary man. An M.D. and a psychiatrist in Vienna before the Second World War, he founded one of the top three (by his account) schools of psychoanalysis in the world. (The other two were started by competitors named Freud and Adler.) Frankl and his family were sent to the concentration camps in Hitler's Third Reich, where Viktor saw everyone except his father sent to the gas chambers. His father died in the camp later, after much suffering, but Viktor survived to see the camps liberated.

Back in Vienna he sat down and wrote his masterpiece in a few weeks. In the book (which is slim, brilliantly written and addictively readable) his theme is constant and firm: everything can be taken away from you except your own choice of how you react to what is happening.

Had it been written by anybody else, that message would still have been extraordinarily powerful, but written by a man who had been through what Frankl experienced, it is nothing less than astounding. One gathers from his other writings that Frankl himself had a strong theist belief, but he doesn't refer to it in this book, and his message places no reliance whatever on that belief. Frankl saw thousands of his fellow prisoners die. He expected his own death daily and came very close to the point of being killed more than once—yet he stayed firm in his view: that the one thing that could never be taken from him was his own personal choice of how he was going to respond.

In a way, Frankl's book is at the opposite end of the spectrum from Rabbi Harold Kushner's *When Bad*

Things Happen to Good People. Kushner's book (thoroughly commendable in its own genre, and of great value to most of its readers) relies heavily on a faith in a divine plan. His thesis is that disasters and vicissitudes can only make sense if you accept the impenetrable rectitude of a divine plan. In that respect, Kushner's book is congruent with the conventional teachings of the Catholic Church and of many other leading religions in which the deity is seen as the architect and puppeteer of human destinies, however veiled and unknowable the heavenly plan is. For readers who lack a strong faith in such a plan, Kushner's book will not help, but Viktor Frankl's will.

Frankl continued his psychoanalytic practice for many years, calling his methodology "logotherapy" (meaning therapy using words), and his theme is one that recurs in most schools of psychotherapy: you, your personality and your personhood are *defined* by your choices and by your responses to what happens to you. The way you react to the world *is* you. Bad and arbitrary things happen all the time—some people get just a few of them, a few people get lots of them and in high doses. In most cases, that is not a fixable or changeable aspect of the world. All we can do is decide how we are going to respond. More than any writer or thinker that I know of, Frankl proved that point in the way he lived through and beyond his experiences in the camps, and in the way he thought and wrote.

On a historical note, Frankl's view of the world has some distinguished and honourable antecedents. His theme echoes the stance adopted by the Stoic philosophers in ancient Greece, of whom the philosopher Epictetus (who also had a pretty extraordinary life and his own share of hardships) is perhaps the best known nowadays. It was Epictetus who, in a book called *Moral Discourses*, wrote that "difficulties are the things that show us who we are." I suspect that Epictetus and Frankl would have got on very well together, had they ever met.

THE CHESS GAME IN THE DESERT

In some ways, then, Frankl's book answers the question about the meaning that each of us brings to our own life and the events in it. Perhaps I can make that point even more apparent with an idea that has somehow become wedged into part of my brain and won't leave until I write it down. It is a rather simple metaphor for human existence.

It seems to me that life is rather like two people playing chess in the middle of a desert.

You can look at the game and say to yourself, This is

totally pointless—here are hundreds of kilometres of trackless wastes and two idiots are playing games with pieces of wood. Or you can look at exactly the same scene and can see in it the intricacies of strategy and challenge, memory, perception, anticipation, synergy, dialectic (two people playing against each other but by the same man-made and agreed-on set of rules) and so on. The meaning you get from the scene is the meaning you bring to it.

Actually, while we are thinking about that metaphor, you could go even further and look at some of the finer aspects of the human spirit in it. For example, the object of the chess game is to win—but you want to win in the right way. It wouldn't achieve very much if you simply pulled out a gun and shot the other person. You'd have won in a way, but you'd be alone in the desert with nobody to play with. Ideally, you'd like to play the game properly and win. Even better, you'd like to win some of the time and lose occasionally, so you know that you are playing chess against another person who has a mind that sometimes works better than yours does. That way, you can learn, and sometimes teach, *and* have the thrill and the uncertainty of not knowing at the start of each game whether you are going to win or lose. The metaphor contains a key to what is worthwhile about human activity while still acknowledging the smallness of the canvas.[1] The meaning of the scene is the meaning you bring to it.

While I was mulling over this point in the book, I mentally staged a quasi-Socratic dialogue between two people, one of whom was a reductionist (a what's-the-point-ist, perhaps) and the other a thoughtful and positive non-theist. The important part of their dialogue went like this (and, like some of the ludicrously stilted Socratic dialogues in Plato's *Republic*, there is a little bit of mediocre buddy-type chit-chat at the end):

Reductionist: Let me tell you what life is, my friend. It's not complicated. You are born: at a place not of your

1. Actually, another example occurred to me, to highlight the smallness of the canvas of human experience. I once saw a television nature documentary about groupers, a type of flatfish, that live deep in the mud at the bottom of Tokyo Bay. They spend their entire lives down there and have very little (if any) knowledge about the conditions at the surface. Presumably if they are extremely sensitive to temperature they might just be able to distinguish an ice age from the current millennium, and perhaps a really hot summer from the depths of winter. Maybe they can feel minor eddies and so might have an inkling if there were a tidal wave above them. But they would have no idea of, let's say, the Second World War, or what type of microchip Toshiba were using in their laptops this year. Perhaps humans have a similarly very limited knowledge of the universe. We guess (sometimes very ingeniously) at what's going on in the physical universe, and we think that what happens on earth among us is very important—even if we also admit that it doesn't amount to a hill of beans.

If we were able to explain their place in the cosmos to the groupers of Tokyo Bay, I hope they'd take the information philosophically. I'd like to think that, at our best, we humans could also accept the knowledge of the limitations of our place. Perhaps the chess game in the desert illustrates the potential of human experience (the glass is half full) and the groupers of Tokyo Bay illustrate the limitations (the glass is half empty)—which is why the groupers of Tokyo Bay have been relegated to a footnote.

choosing, and at a time in humankind's development not of your choosing. You grow up under the influence of the small things around you and of the larger things around them. Then, later on, you die: not usually at a time of your choosing, though sometimes in a place of your choosing. That's it. That's all there is.

Positivist: That is almost a true picture, old pal—almost, but not quite! You have, in a way, described the two slices of bread that sit on the top and on the bottom of a sandwich. The only thing that you have left out is what goes in between them—which is what, after all, makes a sandwich interesting. Birth and death are the inevitable top and bottom of a life, but it is what goes on between those two that actually defines that life.

So let me have a go at describing why life—albeit brief and inevitably circumscribed by birth and death—is still capable of infinite variety and (on good days) fascination and worth.

You are born: at a place not of your choosing, and at a time in humankind's development not of your choosing. You grow up under the influence of the small things around you, and of the larger things around them. That's one slice of bread.

After you have been born and grown up a bit, you can then—if you so choose—fill your sandwich with something interesting and substantial, and perhaps entertaining as well.

Basically, what you can try to do as you make something of this sandwich of your life is to try to sort out: (1) the differences between the small things (the micro) from the larger things (the macro); and (2) those things that are beneficial to humankind from those things that aren't.

If you do a lot of that, your sandwich will turn out to be quite worthwhile. If you do none of it, it won't.

Either way, the sandwich—and you—have a finite life, and as you grow older, you can—if you wish—learn to accept the limitations of life in general and of yours in particular.

Now for the other slice of bread. Later on—at the end—you die. As you say, not usually at a time of your choosing, though sometimes in a place of your choosing. Then it's over.

We have different views of the same object, you and I. You look at that sandwich and say it's not everlasting, it's not immortal and therefore it's meaningless. I look at it and say it's a small and finite space, certainly, but it can be filled with something of interest and of value. And that's it. That's the difference between us, and between our views of what life is all about.

Okay. Now let's go and have a drink.

Reductionist: What's the point? We'll be intoxicated for a moment then we'll convert it all into urine and a headache.

Positivist: True, but we'll have fun for a while. And I'll pay for the drinks.

Reductionist: Ah—that's different. Let's go.

LAST WORD: THE MEANING OF "MEANING"

That dialogue shouldn't be taken too seriously, but the central point is genuine and important—and it is the best note on which to end this short book.

I hope that you've found this examination of belief to be worthwhile. In some respects, all I have been trying to achieve is to make you think for a moment about some of the things that you might have previously taken for granted and never re-examined (which is almost always the way with beliefs of any nature).

What I have attempted in this book is to illustrate how the human species looks at the world. Most of the lessons herein have come from our species' history, our sociology, our anthropology and our neurology. To put it in a nutshell, we are a gregarious, co-operative and aggressive species that has succeeded in colonizing this planet far too successfully. We are overcrowded, and in that situation our natural and instinctive herd instinct—our ability to do lots of Them-and-Us-ing—causes problems, amplified by our abilities to rationalize and to monstrify. One of the precipitating factors of our frequent herd-within-a-herd conflicts is a difference in religious beliefs between two groups. Such differences are particularly likely to be called into play in the preamble to conflict as our aggressive instincts rise, because they concern such vast and significant objectives (or ends) compared with the apparently minor means involved in achieving them. Hence, religious beliefs are an excellent source of intellectual fuel for any growing fire of instinctive aggression.

Furthermore, our brains just happen to be designed in a way to facilitate that process. We happen to have evolved with a brain that possesses a rather fragile right temporal lobe as part of a rather excitable limbic system. In many of us, activity in the right temporal lobe is easily triggered, and when it is, the owner readily undergoes spiritual experiences. Even more worrying is the fact that spiritual experiences can be associated in some people (fortunately a small proportion) with a willingness to kill in the name of god.

I don't know whether the contents of this book will change anything. Actually, I rather doubt it. After all, it is highly unlikely that any slim (and mainly biological and philosophical) book could change the direction of human behaviour. Even in my more manic moods I couldn't expect that. But I can hope that for some people—perhaps a small fringe group situated somewhere in the watershed between the committed theists and the committed non-theists—this book will start off a process of thinking and re-examining. I hope that among all of you who are reading this there will be a few who will at least think again about the whole subject of belief and behaviour.

As I said in Chapter 7, the world would be a better place if we all *believed* whatever we wished but *behaved* towards each other as if there were no external deity to sort out our own problems. So if I can reinforce and strengthen that divide between belief and behaviour and perhaps give some readers pause for thought before they automatically behave in accordance with their beliefs, that will be a good thing.

When you come to the final analysis and try to sum up what we can reasonably expect to achieve in our own brief lives, the main things are all to do with the contacts we make with others. To some extent, it's fair to say that it doesn't matter so much what you believe as how you behave. If you happen to hold the finest theological beliefs there are, and if you understand all the very best and most detailed divine precepts and commandments, but in your daily life you are actually an angry, shouting, inhuman swine, then that's the way you will be remembered. Believing is all very well, but behaving is what you are judged by and will be remembered by. It wouldn't be such a bad old world if we all limited ourselves to treating those around us by bearing in mind the effects of our own behaviour. In fact, that would be a nice way to be remembered.

Perhaps at the conclusion of this book I can recap what I said in another book about the meaning of dying (which, of course, is the meaning of living). I said then— and I still believe it— that "while we live we give a sort of immortality to those who have touched us. When we die we achieve that same sort of immortality in the lives of the people we have touched." The effect that we have on other peoples' lives may or may not be the only immortality there is, but it is certainly the best kind of immortality to aim for.

There may or may not be a god, but whether there is or not, we can still aspire to being good. And that's something worthwhile to hope for.

APPENDIX

Some Books Worth Reading

> "Truth is like daylight shining behind a curtain. All the different branches of human enquiry are like pinholes in the curtain. How much you see does not depend on which hole you decide to look through—it depends on how close to the hole you place your eye."[1]

I read slowly.

I am not (unfortunately) one of those people who can zip through a dozen books a week. On the other hand, I do tend to take a few books and try to suck them dry. So here are some of the best ones.

These books all possess what I call the macro-micro element—they all tell you something about the place of mankind in the universe (the macro, as it were) while giving detail and chapter and verse on their chosen subject (the micro). They have all changed the way I think

1. Attribution unknown.

about some things, and in a few cases, they've changed the way I think about everything.

Ardrey, Robert. *The Territorial Imperative.* New York: Kodansha America, 1997.

Armstrong, Karen. *A History of God.* London: William Heinemann, 1993.

Campbell, Joseph. *The Hero with a Thousand Faces.* Princeton: Princeton University Press, 1972.

Carlyle, Thomas. *On Heroes and Hero-Worship.* Lincoln: University of Nebraska Press, 1966.

Frankl, Viktor. *Man's Search for Meaning.* New York: Washington Square Press, 1984.

Frazer, James. *Fear of the Dead in Primitive Religions.* New York: Biblo & Tannen, 1966.

———. *The Golden Bough.* London: Macmillan & Co. Ltd., 1959.

Hogg, James. *Confessions of a Justified Sinner.* New York: The Grove Press, 1959.

Humanist Association of Canada. *Ten Core Beliefs of Humanists.* Ottawa: Humanist Association of Canada, 1999.[2]

James, William. *The Varieties of Religious Experience.* New York: Classics of Psychiatry & Behavioral Sciences Library, 1992.

Jaynes, Julian. *The Origin of Consciousness in the Breakdown of the Bicameral Mind.* Boston: Houghton Mifflin, 1990.

Lemont, Corliss. *The Philosophy of Humanism.* New York:

2. Copies of the leaflet and further information can be obtained by calling 1-877-HUMANS-1 (1-877-486-2671).

The Wisdom Library, 1957.
Lerner, Harriet, *The Dance of Anger.* New York: Harper & Row, 1989.
Lorenz, Konrad. *On Aggression.* London: Methuen, 1976.
Morris, Desmond. *The Human Zoo.* London: Jonathan Cape, 1969.
Pagels, Elaine. *The Origin of Satan.* New York: Random House, 1996.
Pinker, Steven. *How the Mind Works.* New York: W. W. Norton, 1997.
Trotter, Wilfred. *Instincts of the Herd.* London: Ernest Benn Ltd., 1947.
Wilson, Edward O. *Consiliance.* New York: Vintage Books, 1999.
Worsley, Peter. *The Trumpet Shall Sound: A Study of "Cargo" Cults in Melanesia.* New York: Schocken Books, 1968.

ACKNOWLEDGEMENTS

The idea for this book originated after a panel discussion in November 1999 organized by the Humanist Association of Canada and the Humanist Association of Toronto. The title for the discussion was "Can We Be Good without God?" and it was an article about the event that caught the eye of my long-time friend and colleague Cynthia Good, president and publisher of Penguin Canada. Even though Cynthia's stance on this issue is diametrically opposite to mine, we have both enjoyed our work together on this book enormously. (Perhaps that is the true meaning of the word "dialectic.")

My mainstay from the very beginning of this project has been writer, editor and researcher Michael Schulman—with whom I've discussed every stage in the logical structure of the book, and who also did the spadework on several particular issues. The illustrator is my old friend and workmate Martin Nichols (who also illustrated my book on cancer); his ability to understand what I'm talking about (even when I'm not sure myself) is astonishing. I'm deeply indebted to Professor Michael

Persinger of Laurentian University for his time, effort and patience. Also, I'd like to thank Eve Martin Evans, who gave me some further insights on Joseph Campbell and the hero legends. The copy editor, Catherine Marjoribanks, is a new friend—and I have to say I have been delighted at the level of erudition and insight that she brought to the project.

Like all writing projects, this one stole moments from family life—ones when I was physically present but mentally absent. I need to apologize to my sons, James and Matthew, and even more to my wife, Patricia Shaw, for several such moments—particularly the time in Disney World when I suddenly started getting the idea for the "thunderclouds" picture (see page 204).

So, to everyone who has either helped me or tolerated me over the last few months, I'd like to extend my very genuine gratitude.

Robert Buckman
Toronto, May 2000

Index